MILTON KEY
COUNC
THIS ITEM HA
WITHDRAWN FROM
LIBRARY STOCK
PRICE: SOLD

-- MAY 1997

14

A Blandford
PET HANDBOOK

Small Pets

A Blandford
PET HANDBOOK

Small Pets

Joan Palmer

Blandford Press
POOLE · DORSET

First published in the U.K. 1983 by Blandford Press,
Link House, West Street, Poole, Dorset, BH15 1LL

Copyright © 1983 Blandford Books Ltd

Distributed in the United States by
Sterling Publishing Co., Inc.,
2 Park Avenue, New York, N.Y. 10016

British Library Cataloguing in Publication Data
Palmer, Joan
   A Blandford pet handbook small pets.
   1. Pets
   I. Title
   636′.9   SF413

ISBN 0 7137 1203 3

All rights reserved. No part of this book may be
reproduced or transmitted in any form or by any
means, electronic or mechanical, including
photocopying, recording or any information storage
and retrieval system, without permission in writing
from the Publisher.

Typeset by Megaron Typesetting, Boscombe, Bournemouth
Printed in Great Britain by Butler & Tanner Ltd, Frome and London

Contents

	Acknowledgements	6
	Introduction	7
1	Rabbits	11
2	Guinea-pigs	35
3	Hamsters	52
4	Gerbils	67
5	Mice	77
6	Rats	93
	Useful addresses	104
	References	108
	Index	110

Acknowledgements

The author and publisher would like to thank Mr Dennis Avon for permission to reproduce the photograph on p.74, Mr Marc Henri for permission to reproduce all the remaining photographs, and Miss Anita Lawrence for the line drawings.

Introduction

On how many occasions, when visiting friends with children, have you succumbed to the plea 'Will you come and see my pet' and been dragged by the hand to visit a hamster in an immaculate several-storey housing unit, a rabbit in a hutch or gerbils playing merrily in a gerbilarium? Probably very many! Children enjoy keeping pets and owning a small caged animal provides them not only with companionship and a possible start to a worthwhile hobby but, more importantly, with an introduction to the responsibilities of caring for a living creature and to the facts of life — and death.

There are a number of small animals particularly suitable for children (adults, of course, are by no means excluded from ownership) and the six most popular are dealt with in the following pages. Before rushing out to buy any one of them, however, do make sure that your choice is a wise one and that you are buying your pet in full knowledge of the responsibilities involved.

Hopefully, you will not be choosing a small cage pet merely as a substitute for the cat or dog which you are unable, for some good reason, to keep. In the case of a child's pet, an adult should always approve of the selection and, although children should be taught the importance of feeding, cleaning out and generally caring for their pets, it should be realised that the very young cannot and should not be expected to cope without supervision. Parents must always be prepared to supervise and to undertake the chores in times of illness or other emergency.

It often happens that parents enter enthusiastically into the hobby of rabbit-keeping, gerbil-keeping or whatever branch of the Fancy is chosen and what began as the purchase of a four-legged playmate for a youngster opens the door to a whole new way of life in which both adults and children join a fancier's club, exhibit their pet(s) and, in time, go on to produce and show their homebred stock. To start with, however, let us consider each pet and its main characteristics in turn.

The rabbit

One of the most popular caged pets is the rabbit, which ranges in size from the tiny Netherlands Dwarf, weighing about 1 kg (2 lb), to the big Flemish Giant, tipping the scales at between 5 and 5.5 kg (11 and 12 lb). To give a rough idea of size that is as heavy as a Miniature Dachshund!

The rabbit is easily tamed, especially if you handle and fondle it often, does best kept in a hutch, placed in a garden shed or other outbuilding and, ideally, needs a wire pen which can be moved around on a lawn so that it can nibble the grass and run about when the weather is fine.

Its lifespan averages 7 years; some live only 4 or 5 years, others thrive well into their teens. Maiden does (females) are renowned for their longevity. Incidentally, the rabbit is an extraordinarily clean, fastidious animal, almost always designating a corner of its hutch for toilet purposes.

Figure 1 A Flemish Giant. This is the biggest breed of rabbit and can weigh up to 12 lb

The guinea-pig

The guinea-pig or cavy is smaller than the rabbit, more timid and, in my opinion, more intelligent. It will usually live happily with a rabbit — or perhaps a tortoise — and has similar housing requirements. As you will discover later, however, it has different dietary needs.

There are three main types: the English, which is the most common; the Abyssinian, which is rough-coated; and the long-haired Peruvian. Guinea-pigs live for an average of 3 to 5 years, although some have been known to survive for as long as 9 years.

The hamster

The hamster is definitely a loner. Buyers should never make the mistake of acquiring a pair, believing that they will keep each other company. Even in breeding pairs, the aggressiveness of the female can lead to the death of her mate. As a solitary pet, however, the hamster is a gentle amenable creature. Handle it gently because it is easily frightened and has a delicate bone structure.

Hamsters, for preference, should be caged indoors (or possibly in a warm outhouse). Their lifespan averages 3 years and they make entertaining pets. There is one drawback. They like to sleep during the day and come out to play in the evening and this may reduce their appeal to young children.

The gerbil

The gerbil has made vast strides in popularity in recent years, which is not surprising as this affectionate little animal does not smell, is practically immune to disease and is immensely playful. Usually the gerbil mates for life and, unlike the hamster, male and female are happiest living together. Two gerbils of the same sex can be kept together if you do not want your gerbils to breed.

Gerbils live for about 3 years and again the only drawback to ownership is that they are usually, although not always, nocturnal and, being very small, are possibly more susceptible to injury than the rabbit or guinea-pig.

Mice and rats

Finally, we come to fancy mice and rats. The former have been kept as pets and exhibited for almost a century, the latter for only 25 years.

Mouse and rat boxes (which should be kept indoors or in a warm outhouse) are easily made from timber and wire mesh. Occupants are best kept with their own sex because does come into season every 4 or 5 days throughout the year.

Both mice and rats make intelligent, affectionate pets and it is to be hoped that, as the number of exhibitions increases, the public will stop associating these fancy aristocrats with their unpopular wild cousins.

There are very few animal lovers who have not, at some stage, kept a small cage pet, yet one still hears of many disasters brought about through sheer ignorance: the guinea-pig which died through heat exhaustion or shock; the hamster turned away by a mother who told her child 'I won't have that *rat* in the house'; the rabbit deprived of water because the owner had been told that it obtained all it needed from greenstuffs. These and similar instances which come to mind make it all the more necessary for a book such as this to be written.

In the following pages you will learn more about the pets which I have been discussing and be able to decide whether you would like to keep one, or more, of them. Before handing over your money, however, do make sure not only that you have made the right decision in terms of variety and type but also that you have gone into the commitment in terms of feeding during holiday times, finance and veterinary care. After all, small cage pets ask for very little and they give a great deal of affection and entertainment in return.

1
Rabbits

Origins of the rabbit

It is generally accepted that all fancy rabbit breeds are descendants of the wild rabbit (*Oryctolagus cuniculus*), a creature indigenous to Spain, which was probably introduced to most of their Empire by the Romans. It is unlikely that the Romans recognised the potential of such an animal as a pet, but they certainly appreciated its value as a means of food supply and rabbits were farmed in enclosed warrens.

Rabbits were probably first introduced into the UK by the Normans in the eleventh century and their value as a food animal was again quickly recognised. But it was not until the sixteenth century, when a number were kept and tamed by monks in their monasteries, that the added value of selective rabbit-breeding for fur was recognised.

By the nineteenth century, the wild rabbit population had increased so much, particularly in Australia and South America where it had been introduced, that it had become a serious pest. It was probably the unpopularity of the wild rabbit which encouraged more serious selection among breeders, leading to the development of the sixty or more fancy breeds which are recognised throughout the world today.

For many years, the wild rabbit and the hares were classified as rodents, along with creatures such as mice, hamsters and guinea-pigs. Certain differences, however, led to them being included in a zoological order of their own — the Lagomorpha. The lagomorphs have six incisor teeth compared with the rodent's four; the extra pair are located behind the front incisors in the upper jaw. If you watch a rabbit eating you will notice that it moves its mouth from side to side while it is chewing, unlike the rodent whose lower jaw is arranged somewhat differently. Unlike rodents, the lagomorphs cannot clasp food in their fore limbs.

Rabbits and other lagomorphs have what may seem to us the strange habit of eating their faecal pellets — a habit known as coprophagy. During the day they produce hard dry faecal pellets but those produced at night are soft and moist. The latter are removed from the anus by the animal and eaten when it is at rest. This habit serves much the same purpose as 'chewing the cud' in cows and enables the animal to extract the maximum amount of goodness from its food. I mention this because it is important not to remove the soft pellets from the cage when cleaning it, or to prevent the animal from eating them. If you do, your pet will eventually suffer from a Vitamin B deficiency.

Characteristics of the rabbit

The rabbit is a docile creature, an ideal pet for a child and exceptionally clean, almost always relegating a corner of its cage for droppings. The rabbit will not be at fault if its quarters are not sweet-smelling.

The 7- or 8-week-old rabbit, coming to you newly-weaned, will soon become tame with regular gentle handling. It will even learn to eat out of your hand at feeding time! The older rabbit will take longer to adjust to you and care must be taken not to drop or frighten it. If you do so, be prepared for it to bite, scratch and kick out with its hind legs. But it will only do so when panicked!

You may wish to allow your rabbit inside your home occasionally and you will find that it will quickly accept a cat-litter tray for toilet purposes. If you offer it the freedom of a well-fenced or walled garden, do make sure that it cannot burrow its way out or become wedged in a corner, perhaps between the edge of a garden shed and a wall. This may happen if it is frightened by a dog or cat. These animals are the rabbit's natural enemies and, although with time firm friendships may develop, every care must be taken.

Rabbits are naturally sociable creatures. In the wild they live in colonies, so it stands to reason that, in captivity, they are happier if you can provide them with company. The does (females) almost always live happily together. Bucks (males), on the other hand, are likely to fight. However, rabbits will usually share their quarters happily with tortoises and guinea-pigs. I have sad recollections of my Netherlands Dwarf buck rabbit, which moped and died after the loss of its long-time Peruvian guinea-pig companion. It is so easy to forget that it is not only people who need companionship; that same need is experienced just as acutely by the solitary horse in a field or the rabbit which is left by itself in a hutch and handled only at feeding times.

The rabbit is not generally blessed with great intelligence. It is, however, a gentle creature of habit, deserving of affection and certainly capable of giving it.

Figure 2 The Netherlands Dwarf is the smallest rabbit and comes in several varieties. This Chinchilla doe is pictured with her offspring

Choosing and buying your rabbit

I obtained my first rabbit when a school-friend moved to a flat and bequeathed to me her pet, together with its hutch and pen. Things have changed very little and schoolchildren still commonly acquire their first rabbit in this way, or from a friend with a doe which has kindled who has a litter to give away or to sell. In country districts, it is not unusual to see signs at the gateways of houses, offering young rabbits for sale and pet-shops almost always have several rabbits available.

14   SMALL PETS

It must be appreciated, however, that while any of the above methods are perfectly acceptable, they are rather a hit-and-miss introduction to serious rabbit-keeping. Should you develop an interest in the Fancy, you may well wish not only that you had obtained a better specimen of rabbit but also one of a different variety.

Figure 3 Rex rabbits have a beautiful velvety coat. This handsome specimen is a Self Blue.

Figure 4 A typical English rabbit, large with dark markings on a white ground

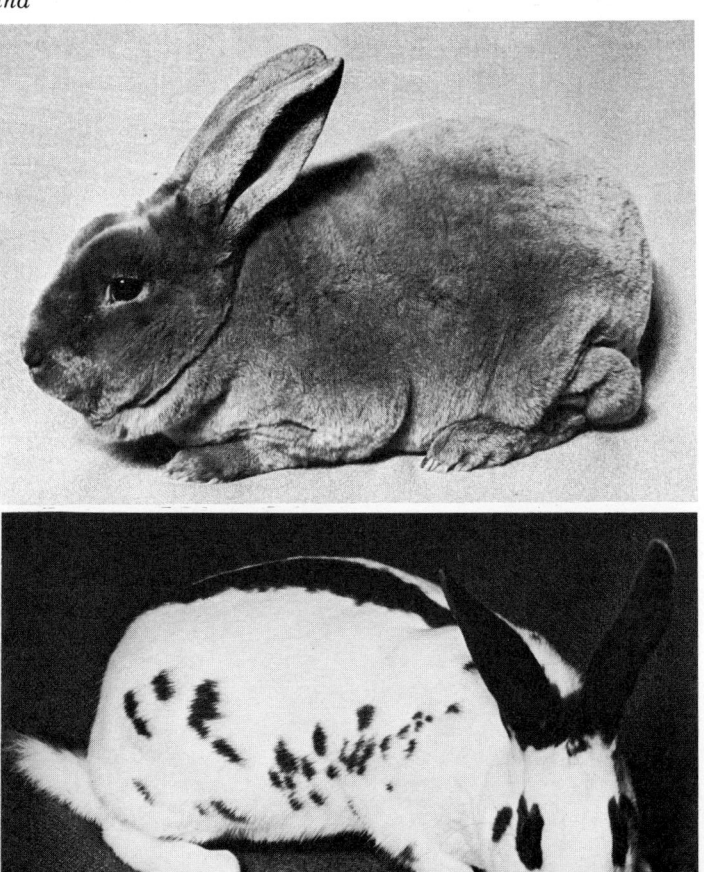

Figure 5 The Polish rabbit is one of the smaller breeds. This is the Himalayan variety

Usually the rabbits on offer in pet-shops are either mismarked, i.e. they differ in some way from the standard of perfection laid down for the variety, or cross-bred, faults which in no way detract from their desirability as pets but prevent them from having show quality.

In most areas, there are fanciers' clubs, details of which can be obtained from a public library or area information booklet. It is worthwhile tracking them down. Contact with the secretary of such a club will enable you to get to know breeders and, possibly, to visit a show where you will see some, if not all, of the rabbit varieties. There are over fifty recognised breeds of rabbit in the USA and thirty or so in the UK.

If you have difficulty in locating a club and/or breeder, write to the American Rabbit Breeders Association Inc. or to the British Rabbit Council (see *Useful addresses*), who will be able to help and advise you.

Until comparatively recently, a journal was published in Bradford, Yorkshire, called *Fur and Feather*, dealing mainly with the keeping of cats and rabbits. This combination of subjects was extremely appropriate as, for show purposes at least, rabbits, like cats, are divided into fancy breeds and fur breeds, and a number of classes even have the same name and coat-type as pure-bred cats, e.g. the Chinchilla and Havana. It would be true to say that the fancy breeds tend to take in those varieties which may have no purpose other than for show, unlike, for instance, the Californian

---

Table 1. Popular rabbit breeds

FUR BREEDS

Californian 4.5 kg (10 lb)	Popular meat breed, white with dark ears, feet, nose and tail.
Chinchilla (Giganta is a large British variety) 2.7 kg (6 lb)	Beautiful dense soft fine fur. The pelts, like those of the South American chinchilla rodent, are used in the manufacture of garments and other accessories. Predominantly bluish grey in colour.
Lilac 3.2 kg (7 lb)	Elusive pale lilac-grey fur, a very beautiful, medium-sized, cobby variety.
New Zealand White 4.5 kg (10 lb)	Popular meat breed, particularly in the USA.
Rex	There are a large number of Rex varieties, e.g. Chinchilla, Ermine and Sable. Some are Self-coloured, others have shaded and patterned coat patterns. Beautiful velvety coat.

FANCY BREEDS

Angora 2.7 kg (6 lb)	Beautiful fluffy fur, or *wool*, which requires regular grooming and is used commercially. Usually predominantly white with ruby eyes. (Four shearings can produce up to 700 g (1½ lb) of wool each year for making hats, sweaters and other garments.)

and New Zealand rabbits which are fur breeds greatly favoured for meat.

Some of the most popular breeds are listed in Table 1. The expected adult weight is included as the larger breeds need proportionately larger quarters than the smaller ones.

Belgian (in the USA, Belgium Hare) 4 kg (9 lb)	Hare-like in appearance but, nonetheless, a long racy rabbit, generally chestnut or tan in colour.
Dutch 2.25 kg (5 lb)	Small, cobby, black and white rabbit with particularly amenable disposition.
English 3.6 kg (8 lb)	Large, well-proportioned, white rabbit with dark markings.
Flemish Giant 5.5 kg (12 lb)	The largest rabbit breed. Black, blue, grey, fawn, sandy or white in colour.
Himalayan 2.25 kg (5 lb)	White rabbit with black ears and nose, tail and socks. Slimly built. More popular on the Continent than in the UK and USA.
Lop 3.6 kg (8 lb)	An unusual favourite with broad drooping ears up to 66 cm (26 in) from tip to tip. A large-bodied rabbit with a bold head.
Netherlands Dwarf 0.9 kg (2 lb)	The smallest breed. A chunky amenable rabbit, extremely popular as a pet and available in a number of colour varieties.
Polish 1.1 kg (2½ lb)	Small compact rabbit, full of fun, generally white, black or chocolate. The albino is the most popular.

You should understand that, in approaching show exhibitors to buy stock, it is unlikely that you will be sold their best specimen. What they may do, however, is let you have one or two promising youngsters, so that you may bring them on and, hopefully, if serious exhibiting is your intention, later breed your own stock.

What you will need

Accommodation

Be sure to know the adult weight of the rabbit you intend to buy so that, when buying a hutch, you can obtain one which has sufficient space.

A small breed will require a minimum floor area of approximately 60 × 80 cm (24 × 30 in), a medium-sized breed, 60 × 95 cm (24 × 37 in) and a larger breed 60 × 125 cm (24 × 50 in). In each case, the hutch should be at least 45 cm (18 in) high. These approximate sizes apply to the keeping of one pet rabbit, so proportionately larger accommodation will be needed if you mean to keep more than one rabbit or, for example, a rabbit and a guinea-pig.

Most people choose to buy a ready-made wooden hutch from a pet-shop. Others acquire a secondhand hutch through a fanciers' club newsletter or the advertisement columns of a local paper. Alternatively, I have often seen hutches among lots at auction sales. Of course, father, if he is a handyman, may set to and make one himself out of a wooden tea chest. A few words of warning! If a secondhand hutch *is* purchased, scrub it out thoroughly with a mild disinfectant before use. If it has housed another animal, there is always the risk of infection.

Some wooden hutches have legs to keep them clear of the ground. Those which do not have legs should never be put directly on the ground but placed on a shelf or table in a garden shed or other outbuilding. Wherever you decide to place the hutch — in a shed or in a yard — the position must be draught-free, with adequate ventilation and the hutch must be both waterproof and weatherproof. Ideally, rabbits should be kept at temperatures ranging from 10–18°C (50–64°F) but they can adapt to a much wider range.

It is also essential that a section of the cage is partitioned off so that the rabbit has separate sleeping-quarters with a measure of privacy. Usually, there is a hole in the partition which is sufficiently large to allow the rabbit to hop through from one section to the other.

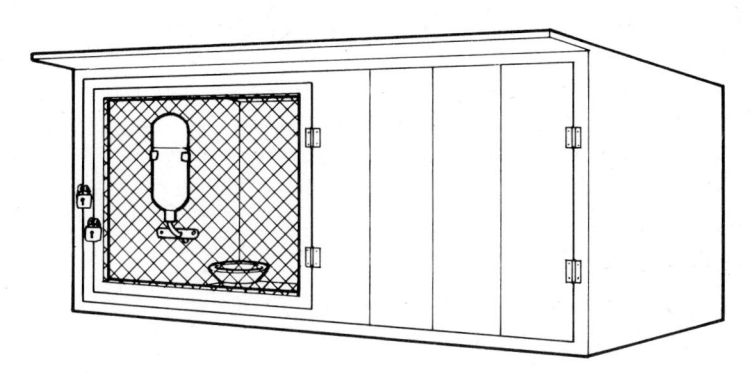

Figure 6 Rabbit hutch showing separate sleeping accommodation, food bowl and water bottle

To facilitate cleaning, you will find that most cages have a mesh front, except at the bedroom end where there is a sliding wooden panel. There should be safety locks as a deterrent to foxes and other predators.

The base of the exercise area should be covered with sawdust or wood wool and the sleeping quarters should be furnished with hay or straw or newspaper. Increase the quantity for added warmth in cold weather.

Cleaning: Hard droppings and uneaten food should be removed from the cage every day. Each week, the hutch should be thoroughly washed out, then rinsed free of all disinfectant and allowed to dry thoroughly before use. Cage accessories and utensils should also be thoroughly cleaned and dried.

Accessories

An essential cage accessory is a branch or sturdy bark-covered log which the rabbit can use as a gnawing block. Rabbits' teeth grow continuously and they will interfere with feeding if your pet cannot wear them down by gnawing.

Other accessories you will need include a water-bottle (this is preferable to a water bowl because it cannot become fouled or overturned), a small, heavy, earthenware feed-bowl or a hopper and, if you wish, a hay rack. The water-bottle, obtainable from all good pet-shops, can be fixed to the outside of the wire mesh either with an elastic band and paper clip or metal strips; the nipple or spout should protrude through a hole in the mesh at a level which enables the rabbit to drink comfortably.

You will also need a scraper for hutch-cleaning and a baby's hairbrush for grooming. A scrubbing-brush, bucket, disinfectant and plastic bags or similar receptacles in which to deposit soiled bedding prior to burning are also recommended. If you are planning to keep oats or other feed in an outbuilding, it is advisable to keep it in a galvanised bin so that rats and mice cannot get at it.

Outside runs

Ideally, the rabbit should be provided with a portable outside run which can be moved from one patch of grass to another as it becomes nibbled. The most suitable structure is a wooden frame covered with mesh. (A puppy run is often suitable.) There are a number of variations, such as a firmly-staked wire netting enclosure. It is essential not to put the rabbit in its run and forget it. It should always be returned to the hutch if the weather becomes very hot or very cold and also at the end of the day. Drinking water should always be available in the run.

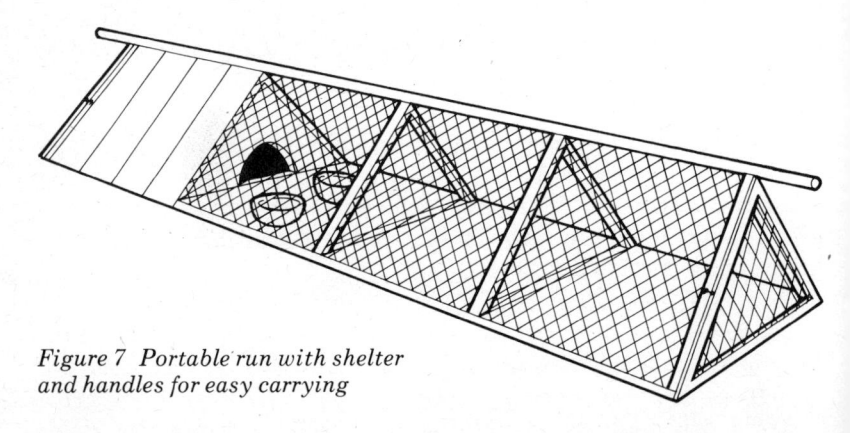

Figure 7 Portable run with shelter and handles for easy carrying

Feeding

There are so many foods that rabbits will eat, it is as well to know some of the things which they should not eat. Dyson, in his book on rabbits, quotes this helpful verse which he ascribes to Mrs Gertrude Latham, the wife of a Huntingdon cleric and apparently a knowledgeable rabbit-keeper:

Do not give a rabbit yew,
Spurge, fool's parsley, feverfew,
Nightshade, purple flower or white,
Lords and ladies, aconite.
Bryony with berries red;
Pimpernels should not be fed.
Add laburnum 'golden rain',
Hemlock with its crimson stain,
Buttercup and celandine,
Foxglove, poppy and woodbine.
If they eat these, rabbits die,
Caution says 'Don't let them try'.

Ivy leaves are also taboo.

Rabbits are extremely easy to feed. The adult requires two meals a day, morning and evening; the main day-time feed should consist of specially-prepared rabbit-pellets (usually comprising a mixture of cereals, animal protein, vitamins and minerals) or a prepared rabbit-mix or similar content. Both are readily available from corn-chandlers and pet-shops. This method of feeding is convenient and saves you having to buy individual quantities of items such as barley, oats, corn and various vitamin and mineral supplements. Alternatively, a nutritious mash can be made up from the following, mixed dry in the proportions shown:

- 40% maize meal
- 30% ground oats
- 10% bran
- 10% best white fish meal
- 10% linseed cake meal

Make this up with hot water or milk to a crumbly consistency and place in a pot of the type which cannot be overturned. A small amount of baked potato peelings or oven-dried crusts can be added to the mash.

The evening meal should consist of greens and include such items as lettuce (in moderation only), cabbage, cauliflower leaves and small quantities of dandelion, groundsel, milk thistle, heather, coltsfoot and clover. Hay is always appreciated and rabbits also enjoy a nibble at garden plants like sunflowers, hollyhocks, marigolds, nasturtiums and asters. It is, however, essential not to overfeed the rabbit with greenstuffs as a surfeit of these can lead to diarrhoea and even death.

If you have fixed up a gravity food-hopper and hay-rack, the rabbit can feed when it chooses but, even so, any uneaten food must be removed every day and fresh food substituted. As a guide, the rabbit which is turned on to good grass will not need as much greenery as the rabbit which spends all if not most of the time in its hutch and which will need 170 g (6 oz) of fresh greens each day. Never offer frosted roots or stale greenstuffs. A salt supply is essential and both rock salt and rabbit mineral lick should be provided and suspended in a convenient position in the hutch.

Health and commonsense care

Hopefully you have got off to a good start by choosing a healthy, bright-eyed rabbit with no discharge from the eyes and nose, a well-conditioned coat and a keen interest in all that is going on around it. If given correct diet and care, rabbits are unlikely to fall victim to ailments. Nonetheless, it is as well for owners to realise that rabbits do not have great recuperative powers. It is the lucky owner who manages to pull a rabbit through after a shock such as breaking a leg, despite the best veterinary treatment.

Handling

Naturally your pet will have a more comfortable life if you handle it properly, which means not attempting to pick it up — as some folk do — by the ears, but by grasping the loose skin at the back of its neck while the weight of its body is supported by the palm of the other hand. The hand rested on the scruff of the neck simply controls the pet's movements. Once it is in your arms and has relaxed you will be able to fondle it gently.

Diseases

The following are points relating to health and diseases which you should know:—

Myxomatosis: This is a fatal virus infection, introduced to Europe from South America, which reached the UK in the 1950s. It has also been introduced deliberately to some countries in an effort to control the wild rabbit population. The virus is carried by fleas. Cases among *pet* rabbits are rare, but vaccination is possible if your pet is likely to be at risk (perhaps by coming into contact with wildlife or even mosquitoes if you live in an area where myxomatosis is endemic).

Diarrhoea: Do not suddenly change your rabbit's diet. Check when you buy your pet what it has been fed on as change can cause diarrhoea.

Coccidiosis: Diarrhoea can also be a symptom of coccidiosis, caused by a parasite infection which affects the intestine and liver. Other symptoms include lethargy, a pot belly and weight loss.

Overgrown teeth and claws: As well as suffering from overgrown incisors (see p. 19 on the need for a branch to gnaw), rabbits suffer with overgrown claws. Many owners trim these themselves but it is as well, initially, to ask a veterinary surgeon to instruct you in the art or you may cut the blood supply to the claws.

Canker: This infection of the ears is caused by mite infestation; a symptom is constant scratching of the ears and shaking of the head.

Snuffles: This is the rabbit equivalent of a cold in the head, which, in severe cases, can develop into pneumonia.

Schmorls disease: This manifests itself in the skin and mucous membranes through external injuries.

The best advice I can give is to check your rabbit every day for any change in condition or behaviour. If anything is amiss, do not resort to home remedies without first consulting your veterinary surgeon. Do not think, quite mistakenly, that he will not want to be bothered with a small caged pet. He will and it is better for you to worry him and obtain a correct diagnosis, than to treat your rabbit for one thing when it may be suffering from something quite different.

Breeding

Sex determination
Determining the sex of rabbits is simple; by putting pressure just behind the genital opening of a young rabbit, a slit in the doe and a

circular shape in the buck will be revealed. In mature rabbits, the vulva of the doe and the testicles and penis of the buck can be seen easily.

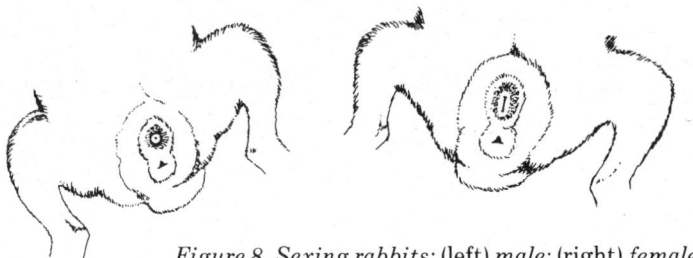

Figure 8 Sexing rabbits: (left) *male;* (right) *female*

Mating

Unlike most female creatures, the doe does not have an oestrous cycle. She can conceive at almost any time if sexually excited by a buck. Matings are, however, most fruitful between January and June.

The rabbit should not be mated until it is between 5 and 10 months of age; smaller breeds reach sexual maturity at the earlier end of this time scale. The doe should be introduced to the cage of an older, more experienced buck and returned to her hutch as soon as the mating has taken place, which, if it is to occur, will happen rapidly. If, however, the doe and buck fight, remove the doe from the cage immediately.

Do not mate rabbits of different varieties. It might be difficult to find a market for their progeny and birth complications could arise because of the size differences of buck and doe. You do not, after all, mate a Pekingese with a Great Dane and, similarly a Lop rabbit should not be mated with a Netherlands Dwarf!

Pregnancy

The average gestation period for rabbits is 31 days although it can vary from 30 to 33 days. The larger breeds usually have the longest pregnancy.

Sometimes a doe will have a phantom pregnancy, with swelling of the mammary glands and the urge to make a nest out of fur for her young. These symptoms last about 17 days. If, at around that time, the doe begins to make her nest, following a sterile mating, this is an indication to the owner of a pseudo-pregnancy. Mate her again at this time if you wish.

Figure 9 An English Lop doe with her kittens

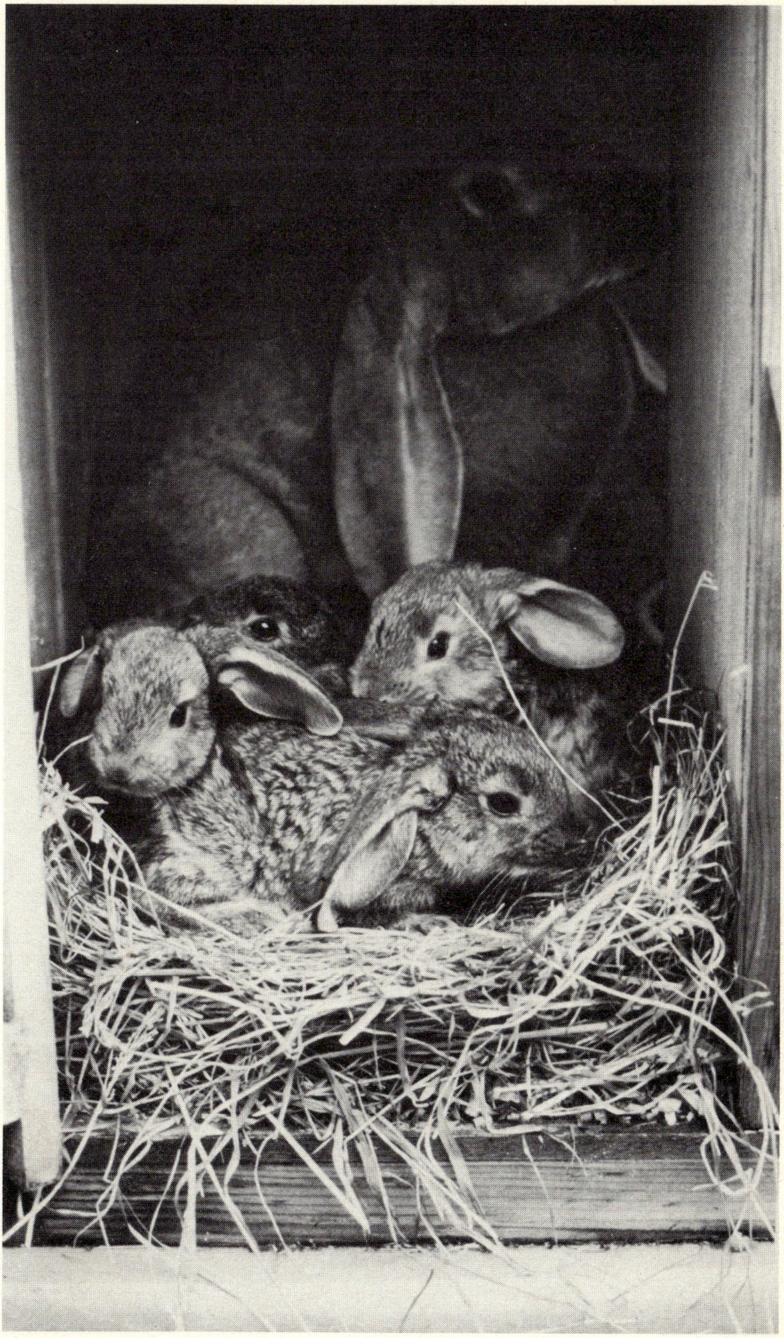

While the doe is pregnant, handle her as little as possible and avoid touching her belly. Increase her food rations and, in particular, her protein supply. This means that the morning meal should be increased rather than the evening greenery until, towards the end of pregnancy, she is receiving double her normal food intake. Milk should be offered and can be soaked in brown bread.

Kindling

About 3 weeks before she is due to kindle, you should put a nest box in the sleeping quarters. A wooden box of about 40 × 25 × 25 cm (16 × 10 × 10 in) without a lid will suffice. Place it on its side and fill it with short choppings of hay. The doe will begin to make a nest from the hay and line it with her own soft underfur. Ideally, a *mesh* lid should be added to the box with a front entrance about 15 cm (6 in) high, which will give the mother easy access and, at the same time, protect her young. She will retreat to the nest a few days before the birth and should not be disturbed. Afterwards you will be able to tempt her out with a titbit to check that nothing is amiss and, if need be, to remove any dead babies.

The average litter consists of four to five young. If, however, it is unusually large you may have to seek a foster mother or ask a veterinary surgeon to put some of the babies down humanely.

Weaning

New-born babies are born blind, deaf and naked except for light fur on their bodies. Their eyes open after 14 days and they should be able to take some solid food at 3 weeks and be taken from their mother and placed in separate hutches at 6 weeks. Do not do this until you are completely satisfied that they are able to nibble pellets and drink from a bottle or bowl.

It is best to separate sexes at weaning, but you can leave this until about the tenth week in the case of smaller breeds, unless they begin to fight or attempt to mate before this.

The show world

The Fancy

Those who are interested in a specific domestic animal which they breed and/or exhibit are referred to as the 'Fancy'. At the head of the Fancy, be it for dogs, cats, rabbits or even goats, there is usually a governing body, in this case, the British Rabbit Council (BRC), which acts as the governing body for rabbit clubs, shows and commercial rabbit production in the UK. In the USA, the governing body is the American Rabbit Breeders Association Inc.

The governing body registers prefixes and it is under its rules that recognised shows are always run. It investigates complaints, upholds the standard of perfection laid down for each variety — by which all rabbits are judged — publishes the breed standards and is the central body referred to by all specialist breed and fanciers' clubs.

Registration

Before showing a rabbit, the owner has to become a member of the governing body. This entails paying an annual subscription and a transfer charge when a rabbit changes hands.

Show rabbits are identified by rings which are purchased from the governing body. These are slipped onto one of the hind legs of the rabbit, above the hock, when it is about 10 weeks of age. As the hock joint grows, the ring remains firmly in position, without causing any discomfort. Different breeds have different ring sizes which are distinguishable by letters (Table 2).

Table 2. Ring sizes

Ring size	Breed
A	Polish
B	Argente Creme, Dutch, Dwarf Lop, Himalayan, Tan, Tricolour Dutch
C	Argente Bleu, Argente Brun
D	Chinchilla, English, Lilac, Sable, all Foxes, Havana, Siberian, Silvers, Smoke Pearl
E	Angora, Argente, Champagne, Harlequin, New Zealand Red, all Rex, Satins
G	Beveren, Blanc de Hotot, Belgian Hare, English Lop
H	Flemish, French Lop, Giant Rabbits, New Zealand White, New Zealand Black, Blanc de Bouscat, Blanc de Termond
L	Chinchilla Giganta, Californian, Alaska, Rhinelander, Thuringer
X	Netherland Dwarf

By registering a prefix, for a small fee, the rabbit breeder, in the same manner as a breeder of pure-bred dogs, can ensure that his exhibition rabbits can all be traced back to his breeding.

Specialist clubs
Most rabbit fanciers are members of a specialist rabbit club, i.e. a club for owners of Chinchillas, Angoras, etc, which enables them to get to know each other, compare notes and experiences and, often, to attend social activities such as an annual dinner/dance, maybe after an important club show.

Most clubs issue magazines and/or newsletters and year books and are certainly of great benefit to the exhibitor starting off in a variety.

The specialist club should not be confused with an area fanciers' club. Often the latter caters not only for those who are interested in rabbits in all their varieties, but also for owners of other small caged pets, such as guinea-pigs, rats and mice, hamsters and gerbils, and holds regular meetings and shows.

Exhibiting
Most varieties need little show preparation. The basic requirement for any exhibit is that it should be in the peak of condition, bright-eyed, with a natural gloss to its coat, which the exhibitor may brush down with a clean, silk handkerchief. The young rabbit reaches its peak at 7 or 8 months of age when, if it has been fed and cared for correctly, it should be in prime show condition.

If, however, you choice has been a long, woolly-coated Angora you must be prepared to groom your pet's coat every day as long as its show-life is to continue.

Something you will need is a well-ventilated exhibition box in which to transport your rabbit to shows. These are made in standard sizes for the breeds and often in double and treble sizes. Advertisements often appear in the Fancy's newsletters and magazines. There is, however, no standard requirement and any strong adequately-sized box with a carrying handle will be perfectly acceptable.

Before use, the floor of the box should be covered in sawdust and a little hay and toast should be put in for the animal to nibble. Do not be over generous with the hay as too much may make the rabbit sweat.

Figure 10 An Angora rabbit being groomed

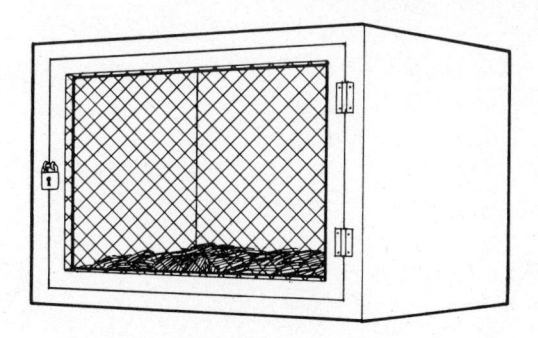

Figure 11 A travelling exhibition box

Judging

It is unlikely that you will be asked to judge a rabbit show for many years and certainly not until you have made something of a name for yourself, exhibiting and breeding a variety and probably serving on a specialist club committee. Many judges have been involved in the Fancy almost all their adult life and can not only see at a glance the rabbit which matches the standard laid down for the breed to perfection, but can also gauge from the exhibits placed before him those which are destined for a distinguished show career and have a chance of winning some of the much coveted trophies which are competed for annually. Don't try and run before you can jump. Study the breed standards and see as many rabbits as you can.

Types of shows and classes

Local club shows are generally what are known as 'table shows'. The owners sit near the ring and, at the appropriate time, take their pet out of its box and up to the judge's table for appraisal. Then there are 'pen shows', where the numbered exhibits are fetched from their pen and taken to the judge's table by a steward; identification is by an entry number on a gummed label in the rabbit's ear. In 'open shows' entries will have been accepted beforehand and, in some cases, sent by rail.

Figure 12 Award-winning rabbits at a pen show

In the case of the larger shows, it is necessary to watch the notices in the Fancy's journals advertising such events so as to make your entries before the published closing date. Care must be taken to fill in the entry form correctly. As a guide, the terms and abbreviations with which you will have to become familiar in order to select the right class(es) are shown in Table 3.

Table 3. Terms and abbreviations

Abbreviations	Meaning
AA	Any age.
AC	Any colour.
Ad	Adult.
AOC	Any other colour.
AOV	Any other variety.
ARBA	American Rabbit Breeders Association.
ASS	Adult Show Stock.
AV	Any variety.
Blk	Black.
B or B	Black Or Blue.
BRC	British Rabbit Council.
Breeder's Class	A class open only to exhibits bred by the exhibitor.
Brood doe	Doe suitable for breeding.
Buck	A male rabbit.
CC	Challenge Certificate.
Challenge Class	A class open to all, or confined to a whole section, such as fancy breeds, normal fur breeds, rex.
Champion	An animal that has won a championship.
Doe	A female rabbit.
Ear label	A small gummed label which is stuck on the ear of a rabbit at shows and bears its pen number.
Guaranteed class	A class in which full prize money is guaranteed regardless of the number of entries secured.
Limit class	Usually confined to exhibits which have not won more than three first prizes.

Member's class	A class confined to members of a specified club.
Novice exhibit class	Exhibit not to have won a first prize at any show, except in a member's class or at table shows.
Novice exhibit and exhibitor class	Neither the owner nor the exhibitor have won a first prize at any show except in member's classes or at table shows.
Open class	Class open to all except where confined to a breed or breeds or to a specified age group.
Pair class	A class for two rabbits of the same variety matched as closely as possible in size, colour, etc. Sex, unless specified, is usually optional.
Pen number	The number given to a rabbit at a show which will appear on the address label sent to the exhibitor and the show pen and also in the catalogue and judging book.
Ring	The method of marking and recording rabbits recognised by the BRC.
Selling classes	Exhibits to be catalogued for sale.
Show (Members)	A show confined to members of a specified club.
Show (Open)	A show open to any exhibitor.
Show (Penned)	A show in which pens are provided for exhibits.
Show (Specialist)	A show confined to its specified variety.
Show (Table)	A show where pens are not provided for the exhibits, each being judged on the table.
Specials	Prizes in cash or kind offered in addition to those offered.
Specialist club	A Society devoted to a particular breed or section e.g. the Angora Rabbit Club.
Specialist judge	A judge recognised by a specialist club.
Stewards	Officials appointed at shows to take charge of the exhibits and assist the judge.

Stud buck	An adult buck used for mating.
Sweepstake show	A show at which the prize money is not fixed, but varies from class to class according to the number of entries received.
Team	Three rabbits of the same variety matched as closely as possible in size, colour, etc. The sex, unless specified, is optional.
Under 4 months	A class for rabbits under 4 months old on the day of the show.
Under 5 months	A class for rabbits under 5 months old on the day of the show.
Youngster	A rabbit under adult age.
YSS	Young Stock Show.

Monetary rewards for showing are rarely great but the excitement is when exhibitors are fortunate enough to be awarded a prize card or rosette.

Sometimes there are classes for Angora products, such as those listed in Table 4, which are exhibited in the London Championship Show.

Table 4. Classes for Angora exhibits

Commercial wool, clipped, 6.4–7.6 cm (2½–3 in staple length (7 g or ¼ oz).

Plucked wool, 7.6 cm (3 in) minimum staple length (7 g or ¼ oz).

Yarn, single, spindle-spun (14 g or ½ oz).

Yarn, twin-ply, spindle-spun (14 g or ½ oz).

Yarn, single, wheel-spun (14 g or ½ oz).

Yarn, twin-ply, wheel-spun 100% Angora (14 g or ½ oz).

Yarn, twin-ply, wheel-spun, 1 thread Angora/1 thread other fibre (14 g or ½ oz).

Article made of 100% handspun yarn (not less than 25% Angora wool).

Article made of 1 thread handspun Angora/1 thread suitable commercial yarn (not less than 25% Angora wool).

Article made from handspun yarn knitted on domestic knitting machine.

Breeding for show purposes

A study of genetics will prove that you cannot produce a silk purse out of a sow's ear and mating two animals of inferior stock will not produce good quality offspring. On the other hand, if rabbits with desirable traits are mated, these traits are likely to be perpetuated.

Newcomers to stock-breeding often become confused by the difference between line-breeding and in-breeding. Line-breeding is the mating of related stock which, if the ancestry is sound, often results in the continuance of a thriving line. In-breeding is the mating of close family members, such as brother and sister, father and daughter, which can be rewarding as long as neither animal has faults as, in such close matings, faults will invariably be passed on.

It is sensible to resort to in-breeding only when you have a first-class buck and doe and want to perpetuate the qualities of both. If you have a promising doe and are anxious to mate her to a suitable buck with qualities which surpass her, you will be well-advised to approach your specialist club for advice. It is also advisable to keep records beginning with the very first mating of your rabbit so that in later years you will be able to look back on the results achieved by specific matings.

2
Guinea-pigs

Origins of the guinea-pig

It is not known from which of the twenty or so species of wild cavy in South America the domestic guinea-pig is descended but it has certainly been domesticated for hundreds of years. The cavies are natives of the Peruvian Andes and were first domesticated by the Incas, who raised them as food animals before the Spanish conquest, a practice which has not altogether been discarded.

The name 'cavy' is derived from the French Guianan word *cabiai* and, today, is fast replacing the description 'guinea-pig'. In any case, the latter is a misnomer because the creature is not a pig. Habit dies hard, however; some members of the public still think that a cavy is a hamster and it is unlikely that the term 'guinea-pig' will fall into disuse for some time to come.

It is likely that the guinea-pig arrived in Europe in the sixteenth century, brought by sailors from South America. It was not, however, until about 1750 that it appeared in the UK, quickly gaining popularity, as it had in Europe, as a pet.

Characteristics of the guinea-pig

The guinea-pig is a fairly large, chunky animal with a friendly, sociable but timid disposition. Its wild ancestors were grassland creatures and so it is not surprising to find that it cannot jump or climb. Some cavies burrow but they are far more likely to plough through the undergrowth. It is not as likely to gnaw as other rodents but, in common with the rabbit, will need a branch to keep its teeth in trim. It is generally much beloved by children who find it affectionate and easy to handle.

In many respects the guinea-pig is unique. It has no visible tail, although there are a few internal bones in the rump area. It has four toes on each fore-foot but only three on each hind foot and grooms itself with its fore-paws but does not eat with them. The sow (the male and female are classified, in common with pigs, as boar and sow) has the longest gestation period of any rodent and her young are very well-developed at birth. Boar guinea-pigs weigh about 1000 g (2¼ lb) and sows are somewhat lighter at 800 g (1¾ lb). Another strange thing is that guinea-pigs hardly ever seem to sleep.

Although guinea-pigs are shy and highly strung, they become very tame with gentle handling and it is unusual for one to bite. It is easy to understand why they have retained their popularity through the years. However, they do become exhausted quickly (never let children fondle them for *too* long) and could easily expire if left out in the heat of the sun.

The guinea-pig has a delightful habit of 'onking' or whistling when its owner approaches. The whistle is also a sign of contentment when a well-loved guinea-pig is picked up and fondled by its owner.

When writing about rabbits, I remarked that guinea-pigs often prove to be suitable companions for them. This is true but, as you read on, you will discover that the guinea-pig, even when kept with a rabbit, still requires individual attention.

Choosing and buying your guinea-pig

Whichever variety you decide to buy, remember it is always better to choose a lively young specimen (about 5 weeks after weaning would be ideal) and to examine it first for any signs of ill health, sores or scars. It should be free from skin parasites, such as fleas or lice, and have no discharge from eyes, nose, mouth or anus.

Young guinea-pigs should be alert and active and run with an even gait. If they do not, this could be due to a spinal or other deformity. Hold out your hand to your prospective pet. It is natural for it to be timid but not for it to run wildly around the cage with fear. It should be well-fleshed, with a firm belly and an even bite. The teeth should not be overgrown. Finally, do not forget to have with you a well-ventilated box, lined with straw or hay, in which to carry your guinea-pig home.

Figure 13 (above) *Self Chocolate variety of the smooth-coated English guinea-pig.* Figure 14 (below) *The rough-coated Abyssinian guinea-pig showing typical rosettes*

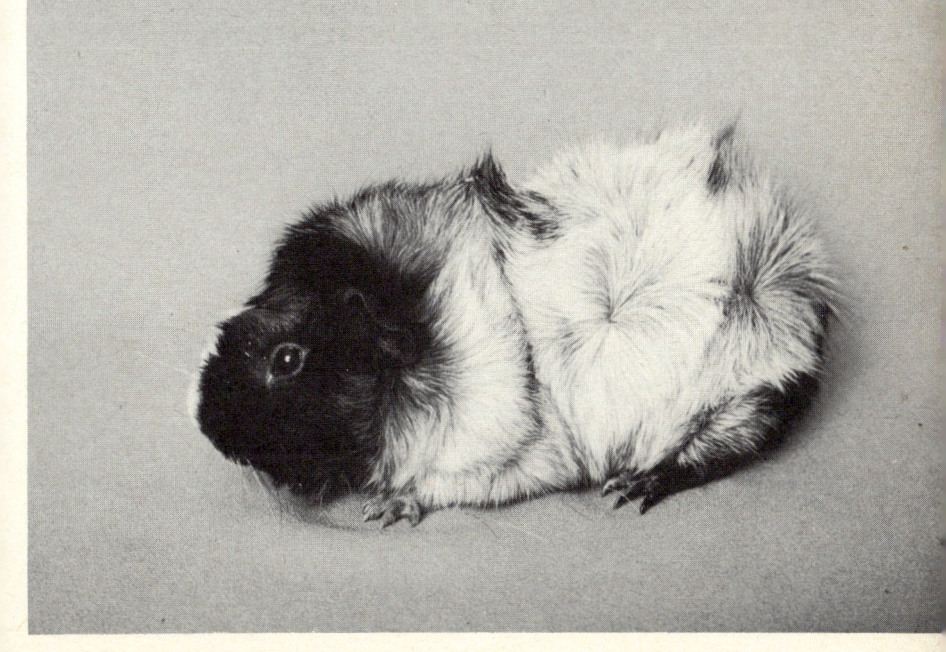

Of the three main varieties of guinea-pig, the English (also known as the American or Bolivian cavy) with its smooth short coat is the most popular and the easiest to breed. The Abyssinian also has a fairly short coat but it is rougher with rosettes of short hair over its body and a crest over its spine. Despite its name it does not originate from Abyssinia. The Peruvian, the long-haired glamour boy of the guinea-pig world, is more expensive to buy and perhaps best left to those with a little experience, or certainly those with plenty of time on their hands for, to do this pet justice, its silky locks must be shampooed, brushed and put in curlers.

Figure 15 The long-haired Peruvian guinea-pig requires a lot of grooming

Table 5. Guinea-pig breeds

SMOOTH SHORT-COATED

Self — Short and cobby with deep broad shoulders and a roman nose. Short silky coat of a deep rich colour all over.

Agouti	Smooth short coat with ticked or speckled appearance due to the plain-coloured hairs being interspersed with hairs bearing bands of two different colours.
Dutch	Smooth short coat, basically white with coloured sections on the head and hind part of the body.
Tortoiseshell and White	Smooth short coat patched with red, white and black. The patches should be square, quite distinct and evenly distributed.
Himalayan	Smooth short coat with a light-coloured body and dark points, like a Siamese cat.
American	Smooth short coat; probably the most popular and well recognised breed in the USA.
Crested	Very like the American but with a white crest centred between the back of the eyes and the front of the ears.

LONG-COATED

Abyssinian	Rough coat not exceeding 4 cm (1½ in) in length, ideally swirling in ten rosettes placed on the shoulders, saddle, rump and hips.
Peruvian	Rosetted long coat, up to 200 cm (2 in) or more, soft and silky in texture, covering the head and face.
Silkie/Sheltie	Like the Peruvian but the coat is smooth and flows backwards from behind the ears, leaving the head clear. When properly groomed for judging, it resembles a teardrop in shape when seen from above.
Teddy	Coarse resilient kinky hair approximately 1.25 cm (½ in) long.

Today, in addition to the original Agouti, there is a wide range of colour variations of each type, some of which are extremely difficult for the breeder to achieve. All three varieties of guinea-pig can interbreed, however, and English/Abyssinian crosses are always popular.

As a general rule, those guinea-pigs of a single colour are described as Selfs, whereas Bicoloured or Tricoloured guinea-pigs are said to be 'marked'. The most common marked coat pattern is that of the Dutch guinea-pig, which is similar to that of the Dutch rabbit. Some classes of rabbits and cats are described by the same name and this also applies to guinea-pigs, e.g. the Tortoiseshell and White and the Chocolate Point and Black Point Himalayans. A large number of colours are also recognised by the guinea-pig Fancy.

As in the case of the rabbit and other caged pets, a guinea-pig may well be offered by a friend and should certainly be easily available from a pet-shop. Once again, however, those offered by the retailer are frequently mismarks, or at any rate unsuitable for exhibition, although there is every likelihood that an obliging pet-shop trader may be able to locate a show specimen for you. What I would emphasise is that, provided the guinea-pigs offered are bright-eyed and meet the health requirements already outlined, there is no reason why, if it is merely a pet you seek, they should not be purchased. If, however, there is the remotest chance that you may later wish to become involved in the Fancy, you would be best advised to locate a local fanciers' club through a library or organisations list, or, in the case of difficulty, by writing to the National Cavy Club or the American Cavy Breeders Association.

What you will need

Accommodation

Guinea-pigs are not as hardy as rabbits. They cannot withstand the same extremes of temperature and should be kept out-of-doors only in fine weather conditions, with the hutch placed in a sheltered position.

The preferred temperature range for a guinea-pig is $16-20\,°C$ ($60-68\,°F$) but, at temperatures higher than $20\,°C$ ($68\,°F$), there is a risk of heat exhaustion. Death can occur at about $32\,°C$ ($90\,°F$) and, because of this, the guinea-pig cannot always be left in a run with a rabbit companion although, if you have a suitably fenced or walled garden, you may, on a hot day, allow it to run free so that it may seek its own shelter among the vegetation.

If they are kept indoors, the hutch should be positioned somewhere warm and draught-free. There should be some light but it should not fall directly on the hutch.

You should provide a well-insulated, roomy sleeping compartment. Guinea-pigs enjoy reclining on a straw-covered shelf about 10 cm (4 in) off the ground. As large a run as possible should be provided so that the guinea-pig can live and sleep in the hutch but scamper in its run in good weather. In the case of the Peruvian and valuable show animals, however, it may be thought best to keep them under cover at all times.

Do not make the mistake of putting two boars together. They will fight, unlike two sows who will live peacefully together as will a doe rabbit and a sow. I have known a buck rabbit and a boar to live companionably but you must look out for the first sign of trouble.

An indoor hutch for one guinea-pig should be at least 60 × 48 cm (24 × 18 in) and 48 cm (18 in) high. For a family group of a male and three female sows, it should be 120 × 60 cm (48 × 24 in) and 48 cm (18 in) high. If you decide on an outdoor home you must make it rat-proof. The hutch design will be similar to that for the rabbit.

The best bedding material is hay, which should be shaken out daily and changed weekly. If there is no separate sleeping quarter, then the bedding should be changed daily. The floor of the run should have a covering of sawdust.

Cleaning: As with other pets, cleanliness is essential. You will need the same scraper and cleaning equipment as recommended for rabbits (p. 20).

Feeding

Should you keep a guinea-pig and a rabbit together, it is vital that, with the exception of greenery, you do not expect the pets to eat identical food. Guinea-pigs prefer foods with a low fibre content. They are unable to form Vitamin C in their bodies so this must be provided in their food. They also have a high requirement for Vitamins K and E. Obviously it is no use buying a packet of rabbit mix or pellets and just filling the food-bowl for two. You must also invest in a packet of specially prepared guinea-pig food, which will contain the right quantities of vitamins, and see that the pets consume their own rations. You will notice that guinea-pigs crunch rather than gnaw their food and that, while they groom themselves with their front paws, they do not use them to hold their food.

Guinea-pigs, in common with rabbits, should be fed twice a day. The morning meal should consist of hard food and the evening meal of greenery. Guinea-pigs also like something to nibble during the day and welcome a little crumbled, oven-dried wholemeal bread, biscuit crumbs or grains of oat, barley or wheat. They thrive best when given liberal quantities of hay, so a hay-rack is certainly recommended. Failure to offer hay may result in the deprived pet pulling out his companion's hair as a substitute!

It is important to ensure that guinea-pig pellets are consumed within a few weeks in case they lose some of their vitamin content, and that they should be given as the sole morning meal only for short periods of time.

Household scraps are useful for making mashes and the recipe which follows forms an ideal balanced diet, full of protein, which is particularly recommended for growing young or the expectant sow:

- 30% maize meal
- 20% crushed oats
- 15% broad bran
- 10% best white fish meal
- 10% linseed cake meal
- 10% meat and bone meal
- 5% mixture of dried skinned milk, calcium carbonate or ground chalk and a little commercial mineralised salt.

Mix the ingredients with a little cold or warm milk, allowing 50—80 g (1¾—2¾ oz) for each guinea pig, plus a drop of halibut liver oil and a multi-vitamin tablet, and place the mash in a dish which the guinea-pig cannot turn over.

The evening feed may include grass trimmings, carrots, turnips, fruit, dandelion, clover, dock, chickweed, cow parsley, hog weed and nap weed, but never offer *fresh* grass mowings. Vegetables which will be enjoyed are the inner leaves of cabbage, spinach, parsley, broccoli, chicory, cauliflower and celery. Peas, watercress and carrot tops are also great favourites, while rootcrops such as turnips, swedes and mangolds are useful during winter, when they should be offered shredded or diced.

Remembering the Vitamin C requirement, be sure to include apples, oranges and kale and, in the case of all vegetables and greenstuffs, take care that they have not been sprayed with any insecticide or contaminated by bird droppings.

It is possible to give a guinea-pig its daily Vitamin C requirement (30 mg) by adding a crushed Vitamin C tablet to the drinking water.

A water supply, provided in a drinking-bottle as previously described or in an earthenware bowl, *must* be available at all times.

Health and commonsense care

Important health points to remember in keeping a guinea-pig are: to watch out for chills, not to overfeed, to keep it away from direct sunlight, and to ensure that it is kept in hygienic conditions.

Handling
You can hold the young guinea-pig safely between your two hands. The correct way to hold the adult is by supporting it with one hand under its hind legs and the other around its shoulders. Be particularly careful when holding the pregnant sow as careless handling could result in stillborn young.

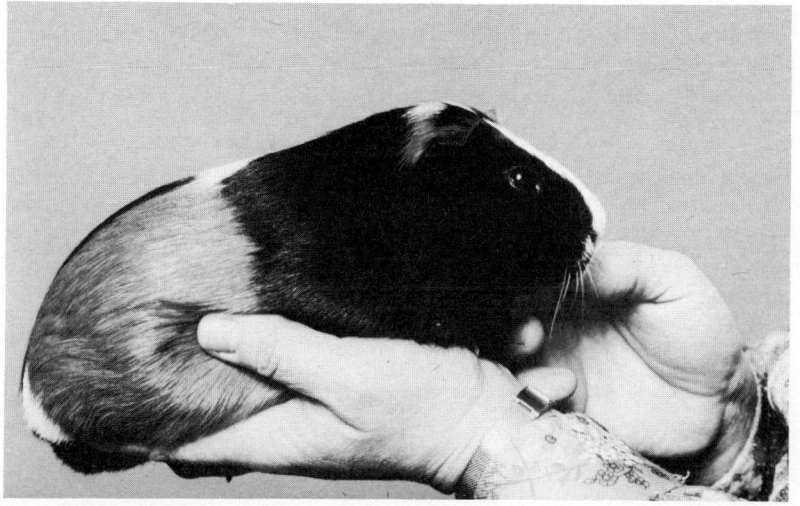

Figure 16 A Tortoiseshell and White guinea-pig correctly supported by its owner's hand

Diseases

Parasites: The external parasites, such as fleas and lice, which are sometimes found on guinea-pigs, may be treated by a non-poisonous insecticidal powder and reinfection can be avoided by general cleanliness.

Abscesses: Guinea-pigs are apt to fight and the scratches inflicted may develop into abscesses. These can usually be treated successfully with a mild antiseptic.

Overgrown teeth and nails: In common with rabbits, guinea-pigs can suffer from overgrown incisors, if a log or similar item is not put in the cage for them to gnaw. Similarly, nails need trimming from time to time.

Scurvy: If the Vitamin C requirement is not met, scurvy may develop.

Respiratory troubles: Guinea-pigs are susceptible to bronchitis and pneumonia caused by being kept in a damp atmosphere.

Constipation: As old age approaches, do not be surprised if your pet no longer has the strength to release faeces from the anus, but be prepared to come to the rescue with a tissue, making this part of the daily cleaning and fondling routine.

If you are concerned about your pet's health or notice any abnormality in its behaviour, do not make guesses as to the cause or indulge in home remedies. Far too many owners have lost their pets through tending them themselves — often for quite the wrong ailment — instead of seeking the advice of a veterinary surgeon.

In the UK, the Zoological Society of London, as part of its hospital, has an out-patients department to which your veterinary adviser can refer your case for diagnosis. However, consultation is strictly by appointment, must be made through your veterinary surgeon and a fee is payable.

Generally speaking, guinea-pigs are healthy little creatures. Given love and correct care, with emphasis on cleanliness, there should be little to cause concern.

Breeding

Guinea-pigs are easy creatures to breed. The sows are particularly good mothers and it is possible for them to have two or three litters a year. You can breed guinea-pigs in pairs or you can provide a boar with three or four sows. Their breeding perfomance will benefit from a high-protein diet enriched with Vitamin E.

Sex determination
You should not attempt to sex guinea-pigs until they are at least 1 month old. Hold the guinea-pig upside down, with its body supported against your own, while you inspect the genital region. Apply gentle pressure with your thumbs on each side of the genital slit. In the male, the penis will protrude. You will also see that the slit in the male is round whereas that of the female is Y-shaped.

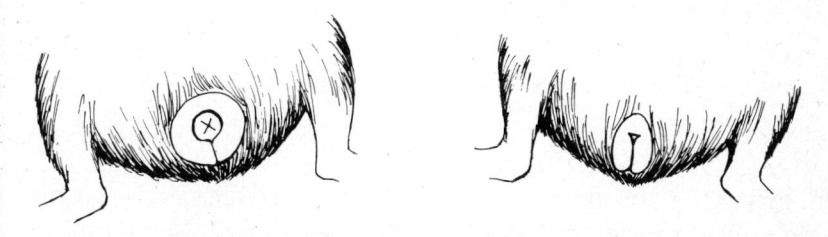

Figure 17 Sexing guinea-pigs: (left) *male;* (right) *female*

Mating
The sow is ready for first mating at 4 months and the boar at 5 months of age. Thereafter, the sow will come into season approximately twice a month (every 16—19 days) for 8—16 hours. It is at this time that she will be ready and willing to mate. If you want to control breeding, as I would recommend you do, the male should be separated from the female as soon as it is obvious that she is pregnant, because she can mate again on the day her young are born. A word of warning — do not use animals for breeding once they are over 2 years old and remember that more than two or three litters a year puts too great a strain upon the sow.

Pregnancy
You will soon be able to detect from your sow's appearance whether she is pregnant because her abdomen will become swollen and, if she belongs to a harem, you will no doubt wish to remove her to the privacy of a maternity hutch. She will need no special materials other than a nesting box and hay. Bread, preferably wholemeal, dipped in milk is recommended for pregnant sows.

Birth

The gestation period ranges from 9 to 11 weeks and the average litter size is three, although seven or more is possible. The babies are fully-furred when born, have their eyes open and are able to nibble solid food after a day. They are suckled for a fortnight only.

Weaning

Although the babies should be eating a finely-chopped adult diet by the end of 2 weeks, wait until they are 1 month old before taking them away from their mother. At 6 weeks of age, the young boars should be taken from their sisters and placed in separate hutches. The sows, however, may stay together until they are required for breeding.

The show world

The Fancy

In the UK, the National Cavy Club (in the USA, the American Cavy Breeders Association) is the body which governs the standards by which guinea-pigs are judged. It is not a pet-club but sets out to encourage the scientific breeding of all varieties of guinea-pig to their standard of perfection and, to further this aim, special prizes, in cash and kind, are offered at the club's shows through the year to exhibits considered worthy of this distinction.

The National Club stages its own annual shows, the Young Stock Show, which caters for all stock under 5 months of age, and the Adult Stock Show, which is for all adult guinea-pigs. The object of these shows is to ensure that there are at least two events every year where every variety of guinea-pig and, in the case of Self guinea-pigs, every colour, is catered for.

Registration

Membership of the National Cavy Club (and American Cavy Breeders Association) is open to all, but while registration of stock plays an important role in the work of the British Rabbit Council, only a limited number of guinea-pig breeders issue Certificates of Pedigree and these are entirely optional.

Specialist clubs

There are specialist clubs, such as the Dalmatian and Roan Cavy Club and the English Self Cavy Club, for those interested in the keeping and/or breeding and showing of these guinea-pig varieties. Details can be obtained from the National Cavy Club (or the American Cavy Breeders Association) by sending them a stamped addressed envelope. Benefits usually include magazines and/or newsletters, one or two club shows a year and, naturally, lots of useful advice.

However, although you may be lucky enough to find the secretary of such a club living on your doorstep, these clubs are likely to cater for, say, a northern and southern region unlike a county (or state) Cavy Fanciers Society.

Exhibiting
Before you prepare your guinea-pig for exhibition make sure that it conforms with the standard laid down for its breed.

In the case of English and Abyssinian varieties, very little preparation is needed as grooming is accomplished merely by stroking the coat with the hand and sometimes applying a baby's soft hairbrush and a toothbrush for the Abyssinian's rosettes. However, if you are showing the long-haired Peruvian, you will have long-since developed a regular daily brushing routine with a brush of soft bristle.

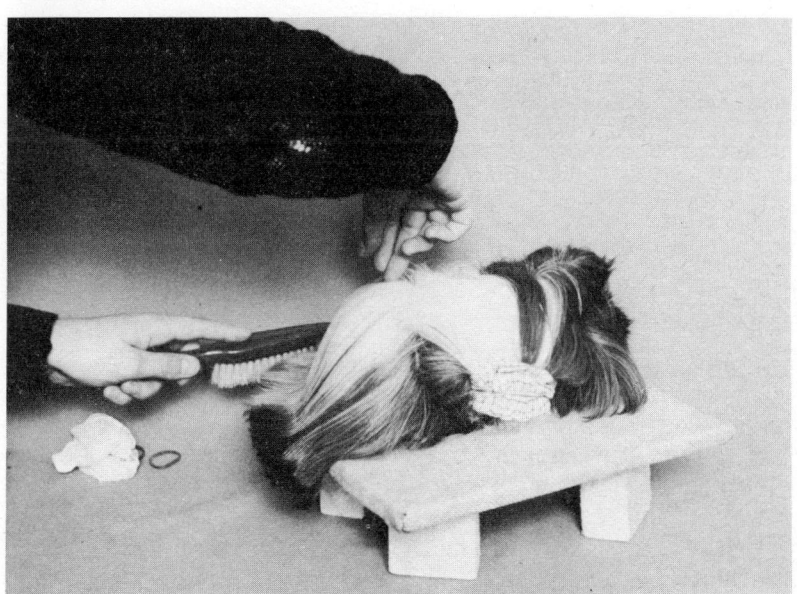

Figure 18 Peruvian guinea-pig being prepared for a show

Guinea-pigs do not usually get very dirty. However, before a show, you may like to give yours a hand-bath using warm, soapy water or a very mild (baby's) shampoo. Make absolutely sure that soap does not penetrate the ears and eyes and that the pet is not returned to its hutch until it has been rubbed down and is thoroughly dry.

You should always brush a guinea-pig's hair in the direction in which it grows; with the Abyssinian you should work upwards and out from the middle of each rosette and from the start of the ridges; work downwards from the head of the English guinea-pig and remember that the glamorous Peruvian should have a long centre-parting.

Judging
In the UK, the National Cavy Club has a judging panel of forty-five members. These officials are elected by postal ballot every 2 years and represent all the important sections of the country. They must be paid-up members of the National Cavy Club who have gained reputations as exhibitors and breeders of guinea-pigs over a considerable length of time. They may, of course, officiate in other parts of the country at any time during their term of office and such judges are recognised by all clubs.

Types of shows and classes
Guinea-pigs are judged at table and pen shows (*see* p. 30). Approximately half the available classes are included in the schedule of a general fanciers' society and the remainder are included at the Fancy's own shows.

Earlier, I stressed that the governing bodies had as their aim the scientific breeding of the varieties and that they were not, in fact, pet-clubs. Nevertheless, some shows do include pet-classes in their schedules and these give the novice owner, and especially the juvenile, a chance to win a prize for the impeccable condition, temperament and appeal of their pet. Therefore, the owner of a cross-bred or mismark should in no way be deterred from involving themselves at least in their local society.

At the top of the tree, however, Championship Certificates are awarded to guinea-pigs securing five first prizes in Adult Breeding Classes (prize money being guaranteed) under three separate judges, be they either National or Specialist Club judges of the breed concerned.

Figure 19 A Himalayan guinea-pig being handled by a judge at a pen show

Judging is carried out on a points system, the maximum available points being allotted to the exhibit which comes up to the standard of perfection laid down for its variety. Table 6 shows some of the classes which you might find in a typical schedule.

Table 6. A typical show schedule for guinea-pigs

Self classes

White *ad*	Golden *ad*	D Challenge *ad*
White $^5/_8$	Golden $^5/_8$	D Challenge $^5/_8$
White $^U/_5$	Golden $^U/_5$	D Challenge $^U/_5$
Cream *ad*	Chocolate *ad*	D Sow AVAA
Cream $^5/_8$	Chocolate $^5/_8$	D Boar AVAA
Cream $^U/_5$	Chocolate $^U/_5$	D Grand Challenge
Black *ad*	AOC *ad*	D Hall Rosette
Black $^5/_8$	AOC $^5/_8$	D Lucky Pen No.
Black $^U/_5$	AOC $^U/_5$	

Non-Self classes

Abyssinian — T/W Brindle	Dutch AC *ad*	Dalmatian-Roan *ad*
	Dutch AC $^5/_8$	Dalmatian-Roan $^5/_8$
Abyssinian AC *ad*	Dutch AC $^U/_5$	Dalmatian-Roan $^U/_5$
Abyssinian AC $^5/_8$	Crested AV	Himalayan *ad*
Abyssinian AC $^U/_5$	Crested AV	Himalayan $^5/_8$
Peruvian	Sheltie	Himalayan $^U/_5$
Peruvian	Sheltie	
Agouti AC *ad*	T/W	
Agouti AC $^5/_8$	T/W	
Agouti AC $^U/_5$		

Juvenile classes

Self AC	Sow	Self Points
Self AC	Boar	Non-Self Points
Self AC	Girl's Exhibit	Challenge Points
Non-Self AC	Boy's Exhibit	Lucky Pen No.
Non-Self AC	Juvenile Grand	
Non-Self AC	Challenge	

Pet classes (exhibits cannot be entered in any other class)

Smooth Pet	Pet Challenge	Lucky Pen No.
Rough Pet	Adult Exhibitor Pet	

ad: Adult; $^5/_8$: 5–8 months old; $^U/_5$: Under 5 months old; *AC:* Any Colour; *AOC:* Any Other Colour; *AV:* Any Variety; *AVAA:* Any Variety Any Age; *D:* Duplicate class for *AVAA* Selfs which must have been entered in one of the previous classes; *T/W:* Tort and White.

Breeding for show purposes
Nobody is going to sell you their best breeding sow, or the most promising youngster that they have. It is likely, however, that they will be prepared to let you have a couple of promising show babies which they will pick out for you and from then on you are strictly on your own. All I can do is wish you luck!

3
Hamsters

Origins of the hamster

The name 'hamster' was derived from the German word *hamstern*, meaning 'to hoard', and is applied to a number of small rodents which are found in Europe and Asia.

The common European hamster is the largest hamster (about the size of a rabbit) and does not make a suitable pet, unlike the dwarf hamster, the Djungarian, which is far more amenable. The Chinese hamster which, like the Djungarian, is grey, can also be kept as a pet, but far and away the most desirable for this purpose is the Golden or Syrian hamster, which is a most attractive and friendly animal.

It is now well known that all the early laboratory hamsters were reared from just three litter mates captured in Aleppo, Syria. It was in 1930 that the Department of Zoology of the Hebrew University at Jerusalem despatched an expedition to Syria to collect specimens of an entirely different hamster, *Cricetulus phaeus*, which was urgently needed for laboratory work. But the seekers found a burrow of *Golden* hamsters, a female and her twelve young, which they attempted to take back to the University. Alas, some died during the journey and others on reaching the University. However, a male and two females survived to breed so successfully that all pet Golden hamsters in Europe and the USA can claim ancestry from the original trio.

It should be pointed out, before going any further, that the Golden or Syrian hamster was identified as early as 1839 by a Mr G. R. Waterhouse, who, at that time, brought specimens back to London

Zoo. However, it was thought that the species had become extinct, until the 1930 expedition found the specimens in Syria.

From then on, hamsters were widely used in laboratories in the UK and France. They first reached the UK in 1931, and the USA in 1938 via the Public Health Service in Carville, Louisiana. Subsequently, when it was realised that they were disease-free and of an amenable temperament, their popularity as pets rapidly spread throughout the world.

As I shall be discussing the various hamster colours and varieties, I should mention that many people feel that the Golden hamster would be better known as the Syrian hamster to avoid confusion now that there are so many colour variations, particularly as it was first discovered in Syria and also because the Chinese and European hamsters were named according to their place of origin. However, the Golden hamster is not, in fact, specifically confined to Syria, nor is it the only variety found there, and authorities believe that this would only result in worse confusion.

Characteristics of the hamster

Hamsters not only make excellent pets but, in common with most small caged animals, are extremely clean if properly cared for. They love to play and budgerigar toys,or even a piece of paper or material, will provide exercise and amusement. They are very busy little creatures and, if given an exercise wheel, will cover quite a few miles racing round it.

They are, however, creatures with a strong sense of territory and two adults, even a male and a female, will be unable to live together in the same cage in peace. In the wild, they are solitary animals except when mating but, even when mating captive animals, care must be taken to introduce the male and female only at the appropriate time.

There is little to choose between the sexes as pets, except that the male is reputed to live longer than the female. He also tends to be lazier and is rarely so industrious as the female in allocating space for a pantry. The lifespan of a hamster is short, ranging from 2 to 3 years, and although cases of hamsters living for 7 years have been recorded, these are exceptional.

Important points to remember are that the hamster is most active at night and that it is not unusual for it to hibernate in cold weather, appearing completely lifeless. Owners often assume, at such a time, that the hamster has died. Of course, in a centrally-heated house, it is unlikely to hibernate at all, but, if it does, it would be as well, before mentally issuing a death certificate, to generate some warmth into the body. This is best done by cuddling the little creature in your hands in the hope that it will revive.

Choosing and buying your hamster

When choosing your hamster, make sure you pick out a healthy specimen. Signs of ill health such as poor coat, dull eyes and wounds or sores are self-evident. It is best to buy one aged about 8 to 10 weeks. A hamster may not be tame at this age, but it will soon get used to being handled, besides which, if you buy a youngster, you should be able to enjoy its company for longer.

Where you buy depends largely on the purpose for which the pet is intended. If you are looking merely for an entertaining companion to love and look after, there is likely to be an attractive, healthy specimen waiting for you at the nearest pet-shop. If, however, you plan to go in for hamsters on a hobby basis, beginning by joining an area fanciers' club, getting to know other owners and later exhibiting, it would certainly be a good idea to locate a few breeders first of all and, if possible, to attend one or two shows, so that you have a good idea of the types of animal available. In this way, you can avoid making a hasty choice and being disappointed later when you perhaps see another variety which you would have preferred.

When one talks of the Golden hamster, there are more than thirty colour varieties recognised by the National Hamster Council in Britain alone, including Golden, Honey, Beige, Cinnamon, Grey, Blonde and White. Some can have black or ruby eyes and they may be Piebald, Satin, Rex, Long-haired or what is known as 'Banded' where, for instance, the pet is white with a cinnamon band. There are also Tortoiseshells and Mosaics, although at the time of writing no show standard exists for the latter.

The European hamster is not suitable as a pet. Not only is it a rare endangered species which, in the UK, can only be imported under a Department of the Environment licence, but it is also a biter. It weighs 200–300 g (7–10½ oz) compared with the 100–150 g (3½–5¼ oz) of the Syrian variety. It originates from the steppes in eastern Europe, is light brownish yellow on top becoming a dark and reddish brown on the head, with this colour running into a band round the chest. Cheeks and wrists are white, the underside of the legs is mostly black and the forehead stripe is black.

It is possible, however, to obtain a Chinese hamster as a pet; this species originates from China and Mongolia. This species is 7.5−12.5 cm (3−5 in) long and has a longer tail than the Syrian hamster, whose tail is very short indeed, or the European hamster which has a short but very noticeable tail. The Chinese hamster is greyish brown in colour with a black dorsal stripe and a whitish belly. The Chinese Dwarf hamster also has a black dorsal stripe which, in the wild, turns completely white in winter to prevent being seen in the snow.

What you will need

Accommodation
Hamsters should have quarters which are easily cleaned and positioned in a draught-free area where there is adequate light and ventilation. An even temperature of 16−20°C (61−72°F) is preferable, with normal hours of light and darkness, and, because of their solitary nature, all adults must be kept in separate cages.

There are numerous types of hamster cages but many of those available are too small. Hamsters, at night, are very active creatures. They need space in which to climb, play, move their bedding about and feed. There is, however, no need to provide a separate sleeping compartment as, if given the right materials, the animal will make its nest in full view, a habit which is obviously to the owner's advantage as the pet can be seen during the daytime.

Soft meadow hay makes the best bedding (straw and cotton wool can be harmful) and the cage floor should have a covering of sawdust which should be cleaned out and replaced at least once a week. The nest materials need not be replaced unless it becomes very soiled.

Hamsters quickly learn to deposit their droppings in one place. Indeed, a jar containing a small portion of soiled litter, placed in a corner of the cage, will encourage the pet to adopt the receptacle for toilet purposes.

The pen may be constructed of wood, metal or plastic. If wood is used, however, precautions must be taken against the gnawing habit of hamsters. The wood must be well-seasoned hardwood at least 1.5 cm (⅝ in) thick. The interior should be painted with a non-poisonous hard gloss paint. Any tempting edges should have a metal strip attached. The joint should be flush fitting. These precautions, together with the extra precaution of giving the animal something to gnaw, should prevent trouble.

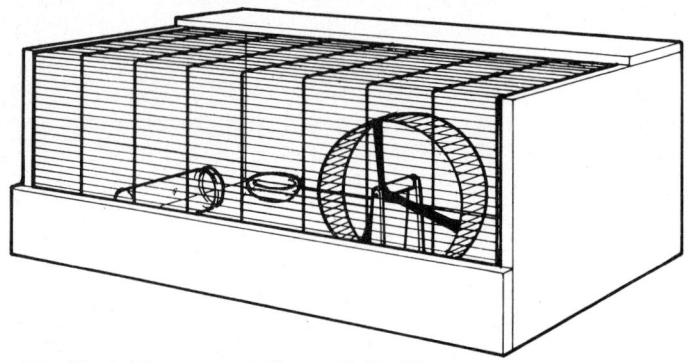

Figure 20   Typical commercially available hamster cage, showing exercise wheel, toilet jar and food bowl

An alternative system of hamster housing is the Rotastak method, an exciting idea which provides a more natural environment for your pet. The starter unit makes a complete home in itself but Rotastak has been designed to be extensible — upwards, downwards and outwards, making it more fun for you and your pet. Hamsters in their natural environment live in networks of underground burrows and Rotastak has been created with this very much in mind. Translucent tubes are used to form 'burrows', so that while your pet enjoys more freedom you can always see it. From the basic starting unit, which consists of the living compartment and loft connected by a tube, the Rotastak enthusiast can build up a complete network of housing. Individual compartments or sections can be sealed off so that your pet can be confined to part of the system during cleaning operations.

You can buy this system in individual units from most good pet-shops and, in the UK, there is a Rotastak National Hamster Club, membership of which is free to anyone who wishes to join, regardless of whether they own a Rotastak unit. Answers are given to members on all hamster queries.

Yet another type of hamster cage is of the bird-cage variety on a standard lamp-style base, although I fear that some of these cages have been designed for their aesthetic appeal rather than their housing value.

Whatever the accommodation you provide for your hamster, it is extremely important that it should be escape-proof. Indeed, in the USA, the Department of Agriculture has issued a warning to this effect to hamster-breeders in case escaped hamsters should establish colonies in the wild and create a rodent problem as they are destructive to crops and agriculture. This is unlikely to happen in the UK because the climate is not suitable for breeding.

Accessories

Having bought your cage and prepared the bedding, you will have realised that, being a solitary creature, your hamster will want something to amuse itself with and that items such as ramps, ladders, logs, cotton reels and even nuts will provide acceptable diversions. If dishes have not been provided with your cage, you should obtain a small, non-capsizable food-bowl, preferably one of the hopper variety, which will ensure that an adequate supply of food, and no more, is constantly available; also a water-bowl, again sufficiently heavy to avoid being capsized, or a water-bottle, with dripper, which can be fixed to the cage.

Figure 21 Hamster exercising in its wheel

Feeding

A balanced diet is essential if hamsters are to be kept in peak condition. They will eat almost anything but it is better to feed them on either a mash or a mixture of grain and green vegetables.

The mash, comprised of table scraps of meat, egg and fish, biscuit and cooked vegetables, should be firm and crumbly and the amount provided should be sufficient for one day's meal only. Hamsters store excess food and a mash of this type would go mouldy.

An alternative diet is mixed corn supplemented whenever possible by fresh green and root vegetables. In either case, fresh milk as well as drinking water should be provided. Whole oats in husks should be avoided since their sharp tips could injure or even penetrate the lining of the hamster's cheek pouches, causing a nasty wound.

It is not generally realised that hamsters are not completely vegetarian and that they relish titbits of mealworms, earthworms, moths or caterpillars.

Figure 22 Himalayan variety of hamster feeding

Of course, it is possible to obtain packets of specially prepared hamster food in the form of pellets from pet-shops, but if you use these, do make sure that they are supplemented with fresh foods.

As a guide, the total quantity of food which will be consumed by a hamster in one day is little more than a tablespoonful. A few drops of cod liver oil added to its milk are beneficial and do remember that unclean food or overfeeding can cause digestive disorders.

Health and commonsense care

Hamsters are remarkably healthy, disease-free animals; most ailments result from bad husbandry, such as incorrect feeding and housing. Daily inspection should enable you to detect anything unusual in your pet's appearance and behaviour. A sick hamster should be transferred immediately to another cage with clean bedding.

Handling
Remember that hamsters are timid creatures and should not be startled or suddenly awakened from sleep. Let your hamster see your hand approaching it, stroke it before you lift it and, as you do so, cup it gently in your hands.

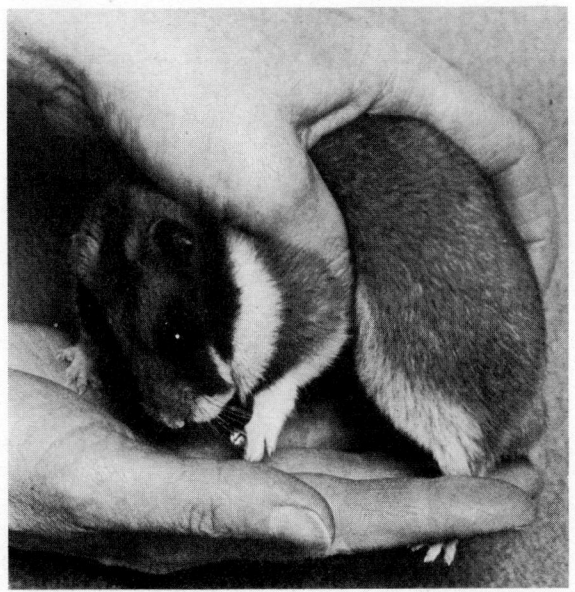

Figure 23 Golden hamster being lifted correctly

It is possible to pick up an untamed hamster by the scruff of its neck so that it cannot wriggle round and bite the handler, but this method is definitely not advocated for a pet and should not be adopted as a matter of course.

Do not become concerned if you detect a spot on the hips of your pet. These are scent spots which warn off other hamsters in the wild and not an ailment or blemish.

Diseases

Parasites: Parasites, such as lice and fleas, sometimes occur and should be treated with flea powder, one of the several on the market for cats and dogs is suitable. Apply powder to the cage and surround every 3 or 4 days and remember to give a complete change of bedding afterwards in case any remaining eggs hatch.

Respiratory troubles: The complaints from which hamsters most frequently suffer are colds and pneumonia, indicated by listlessness and slow, wheezy breathing. *Colds can be picked up from humans* and, if neglected, pneumonia will follow. The hamster's tendency to develop pneumonia makes it particularly important for the owner to provide warmth and ventilation.

Injuries: Falls may result in bone fractures or internal injuries and if this happens immediate veterinary assistance should be sought. Hamsters are excellent at cleaning small wounds themselves and these heal amazingly quickly. However, it is always best to seek qualified help.

Teeth: Something for the hamster to gnaw is essential. If teeth or claws grow too long or have broken you can attend to these carefully with a pair of nail scissors.

Wet-tail: This is a highly contagious type of diarrhoea, resulting in a messy discharge around the tail. Alas, it is usually fatal. It can occur in hamster colonies but should not occur in pet hamsters. Other signs are listlessness, loss of appetite and lack of sheen on the coat. Isolation and disposal of the cage contents are essential. Do not give up hope. Your veterinary surgeon will try and save your pet if he possibly can.

Cage paralysis: This is a distressing condition in which the pet is unable to raise its head and pushes its nose on the floor. It is caused by lack of Vitamin B and can be cured by exercise and adding a few drops of cod liver oil to the feed.

Breeding

Before attempting to breed hamsters, you must appreciate that a number of cages will be required, one each for the male and female and also for the young. The breeding cage can be of the same type as the normal cage with a floor space of 60 × 30 cm (24 × 12 in). Ample protein in the diet and the addition of half a teaspoonful of wheat-germ to their daily rations will help to keep your hamsters in tiptop breeding condition.

Sex determination

The sex of a hamster can be determined by the shape of its rear end. The male has an elongated hind end and there is a prominent bulge just before the tail whereas the female is more rounded and has no bulge. Females can also be recognised, up to the age of about 8 days while they have no fur, by the two rows of teats along the abdomen.

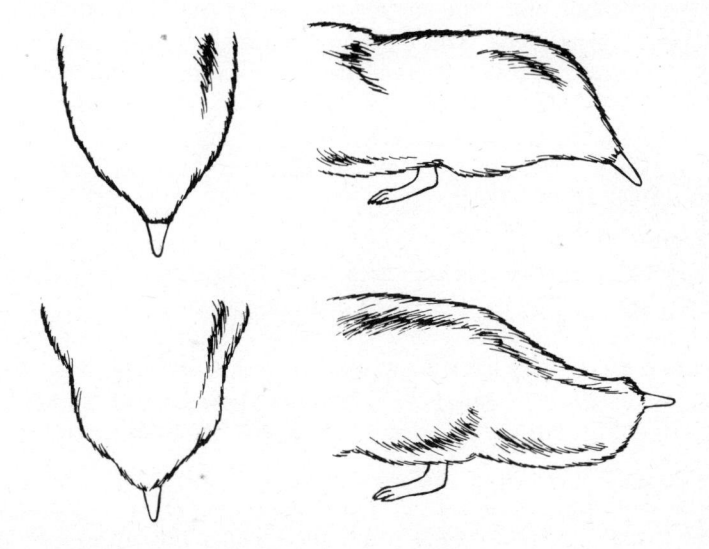

Figure 24 Sexing hamsters: (above) *female;* (below) *male*

Mating

Hamsters will breed from as early as 5 weeks but it is better for the female to be between 12 and 20 weeks old when she has her first litter. The male can be younger but not less than 8 weeks old. Do not mate animals over 1 year old. Hamsters may breed at any time of the year but April to October matings are the most successful. Male hamsters are usually ready to mate at any time. Female hamsters have a breeding or oestrus cycle of 4 days. The cycle is usually repeated continuously as long as the female is in breeding condition. Successful mating can occur on the evening of only one of these 4 days. The beginner, therefore, will have to rely on putting the male and female together on successive evenings in order to be reasonably sure of success.

When breeding hamsters, you must be aware that the aggressiveness of the female towards the male can lead to severe injury or even death. Sometimes it is possible to rear hamsters in mated pairs from weaning (25 days onwards) but it is a method not to be recommended. It is far better to establish pairs only when mating is required.

Introductions are best made gradually. This may be achieved by putting the male in the female's cage and the female in the male's cage for short periods of time. Next, return the pair to their respective cages but place the cages together so that the hamsters may inspect one another. You may now place the female in the male's cage (never the other way around) for about 20 minutes before returning her to the familiarity of her own home. Watch the pair carefully while they are together in case they begin to fight and be prepared, by wearing stout gloves, to separate them if necessary.

Pregnancy

The gestation period is 15–17 days (the shortest of any mammal). Pregnant females require extra protein, greens and milk. On about the eleventh day of pregnancy, the cage should be cleaned out and extra materials for bedding provided so that the expectant mother can make her nest. An open-topped nest-box with a floor area of 15 × 15 cm (6 × 6 in) can be provided but this is not essential.

Birth

The litter usually consists of about 7 young but up to 12 may be born. They are born naked and blind. Their eyes open when they are

14 days old. After the birth, increase the mother's rations so that the babies can have a good start. Make no attempt to disturb the babies for a fortnight, except for carrying out the usual cage-cleaning. Mother hamsters resent interference in these early days and premature inspection can only put the lives of the baby hamsters at risk.

Figure 25   Litter of young Cream hamsters

Weaning
The young hamsters will start to eat dry food when they are 5—8 days old. A mixture of fine oatmeal is suitable and at 10 days they can manage some chopped green food. Male and female offspring must be segregated when they are 4 or 5 weeks old and homes found for them. The mother should be removed when the young are about 25 days old.

The show world

The Fancy
In the UK there is a governing body, the National Hamster Council, under whose rules hamsters are judged.

In the USA, there are many hamster clubs and questions regarding governing bodies would be best directed to the Animal Care Staff of the Animal and Plant Health Inspection Service (see *Useful addresses*).

There are three regional hamster clubs in the UK: the Southern Hamster Club, which covers all of the southern counties of England; the Midland Hamster Club, which covers the Midland counties and Wales; and the Yorkshire Hamster Club which covers the northern counties and Scotland. The three clubs are all affiliated to the National Hamster Council which lays down the standards for the various colour varieties and also sets the regulations for exhibiting.

The three clubs have been in existence for approximately 30 years and all members receive a monthly magazine entitled *The National Hamster Council Journal*.

Judging

The governing body lays down the judging standard for each variety and it is up to the Council to decide if, and when, a newly declared type is to be officially recognised.

Basically a judge, according to NHC rules, looks for: 'a hamster of good size, with a broad, rounded skull on a large head, and with a short, blunt, unratlike face. Ears should be large, set well apart and upstanding when the hamster is awake. The fur should be soft, short and dense, except in the case of long-haired hamsters. In the long-haired variety, the hair should be long, soft and fine in texture'.

Judging is carried out under a points system, with a grand total of 100 for the perfect hamster which gains the maximum obtainable points for colour, markings, fur, size, condition, eyes and ears. Penalties are awarded for overweight, scars, sores and wounds or being shown in an unclean cage. Disease obviously means disqualification.

Types of shows and classes

Classes are held for all the recognised colours and types and sometimes also for pet hamsters, but obviously the range of these varies from the limited number that might be included in a general fanciers' club show to the full range at a Hamster Club show. If in doubt about which classes to enter, it is as well to have a word with the show secretary well beforehand. Table 7 is an example of classes at a hamster championship show.

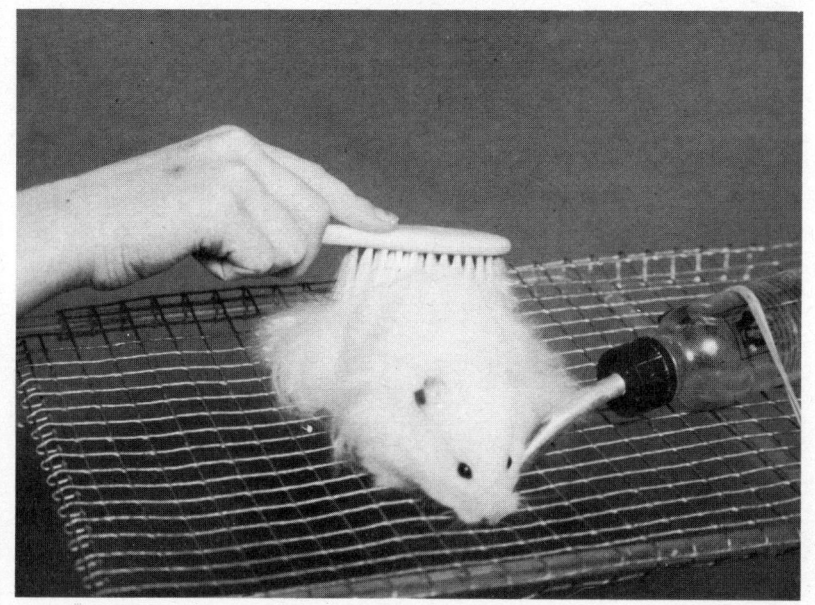

Figure 26 Grooming a White Long-haired hamster

Table 7. Classes at a hamster championship show

1. Golden
2. Black-eyed Cream (male)
3. Black-eyed Cream (female)
4. White
5. Cinnamon
6. Grey
7. Any Other Colour (standard)
8. Satin (male)
9. Satin (female)
10. Long-haired male
11. Long-haired female
12. Satin long-haired male
13. Satin long-haired female

Duplicate classes

14. Junior Exhibitor (Armitage Bros. Challenge Cup Class)
15. Breeders (exhibit to have been bred by exhibitor)
16. London Ch. Show Society Members Class
17. GRAND CHALLENGE

Breeding stock for show purposes

As with any pet it is essential to breed from sound foundation stock, purchased from a proven and reliable exhibitor or breeder. In the case of hamsters, colour may be foremost on your mind, so it is essential that the stock you buy comes from a true colour line.

4
Gerbils

Origins of gerbils

Gerbils are tiny members of the rodent family and are related to hamsters, lemmings and voles. In size they come somewhere between a mouse and a rat.

There are more than 100 known species of gerbils, jirds and related animals. The majority are small, sandy-coloured creatures with long, slightly furry tails. The jerboas of Africa and India and the kangaroo rats of North America have conspicuously long back legs and move in a series of hops, holding the short front legs clear of the ground. The back legs of both gerbils and jirds are not so long and they move on all fours.

In the wild, gerbils and jirds live in the more arid areas of eastern Europe, also in the deserts, savannas and sandy grasslands of much of Africa and Asia, where they dig burrows as an escape from the intense heat of the dry season. They can, in periods of drought, survive considerable periods without drinking, relying instead on the moisture in their diets which, in the wild, include roots, seeds, tubers, bulbs, insects and, in some species, small eggs and nesting birds.

It appears to have been in 1866 that Père David, a French naturalist, seeing the Mongolian gerbil for the first time during his travels through Mongolia and China, recorded the following words in his diary: 'This morning I acquired . . . three yellow rats I do not yet know the name of, having long, hairy tails . . .'. Specimens of the yellow rats were sent by Père David to the Paris Museum of Natural

History, where they were classified by Henri Milne-Edwards under the Latin name *Meriones unguiculatus*. *Unguis* is the Latin word for 'claw' whereas *Meriones* was the name given to a Greek warrior who had tusks on his helmet.

Characteristics of gerbils

We do not know who first recognised pet potential in the gerbil but whoever it was is to be congratulated for gerbils have virtually no fear of man, are practically immune to disease, free from odour, easily tamed, able to tolerate a wide range of temperature and have little tendency to bite or, indeed, escape. In all, they make delightful and entertaining companions for people of all ages, the only possible drawback being that they should not be played with by *very* small children lest, through mishandling, the creatures should be hurt because of their very small size.

Another great asset in keeping gerbils is that, unlike the hamster, a solitary creature which must be kept alone, gerbils live happily in pairs and two members of the opposite sex or sisters may be kept together, although two males are quite likely to fight. A solitary gerbil would be a lonely one.

Training is virtually unnecessary. These bold affectionate animals soon get to know their owners and will eat from their fingers. Indeed the gerbil that has known its owner from weaning may become sufficiently tame to climb onto their shoulders. A few words of warning: never handle a gerbil to the exstent that it becomes exhausted. When you see a gerbil lying stretched out and trembling you know it is high time for it to be returned to its cage!

Choosing your gerbil

Although there are many species of gerbils, jirds and related rodents there are only two, possibly three, species which make good pets. The most suitable are the Mongolian gerbil and the Libyan gerbil.

The Mongolian gerbil is a small, friendly animal with fairly thick fur, small ears, black nails on its toes and hairy soles to its feet. The body of the adult measures about 10 cm (4 in) and the tail is slightly shorter than the body. Even when it is unaccustomed to being handled the Mongolian gerbil very rarely bites and it adapts to human care very quickly.

The Libyan gerbil is very similar to the Mongolian gerbil except that it is larger, 12—15 cm (5—6 in) long, and has white toenails. Again, it is a creature of friendly disposition, very easily tamed.

The third species sometimes offered for sale is the Naked Soled gerbil, *Tatera indica*. This is a rather unattractive, rat-like animal and is probably best avoided since it is fairly difficult to tame. It can be distinguished from the other two species by the absence of fur on the soles of the feet and by the tail, which is longer than the body.

The Mongolian gerbil is slightly smaller, and the Libyan gerbil slightly larger, than the Golden hamster, the males being half as large again as the females. They have golden brown fur shading to white underneath with some long black hairs on the back. There are five toes to each foot and the easiest way to tell the two species apart is by the colour of the claws (pp. 68—9). However, the Mongolian gerbil is far and away the most popular pet and if you set out to buy a gerbil, or wish to exhibit, it is likely that this is the species you will wish to purchase.

There are not as yet a great many varieties from which to choose and most of those kept as pets vary little in colour from their wild counterparts. There are three colour types which are classified as breeds: a) the Albino, whose white skin and fur and pink eyes are due to lack of pigment, a condition known as albinism which often appears in the early days of any breeding programme, b) the Black, a mutation which occurred in the USA and was imported into the UK, and c) the Cinnamon, another breed developed in the early days, which has a pale, short coat lacking the characteristic long dark guard hairs. Other rare colour varieties are mentioned in Table 8.

My initial advice on choosing a gerbil would be to locate a fanciers' society in your area, get to know a few breeders and, if possible, attend some shows before making your selection. If, however, you do not aspire to joining the Fancy but wish merely to acquire a couple of entertaining companions, I am sure that your nearest pet-shop will be able to help you.

What you will need

Accommodation

Gerbils need warmth and must be kept indoors, away from damp and where the temperature is about 20—24°C (68—75°F). Excessive heat must be avoided.

Gerbils are ground-living animals so, although the cage need not be high, it should have a reasonable floor area. For a pair of gerbils, a normal hamster cage approximately 40 × 20 cm (16 × 8 in) is adequate. If you can provide more space, so much the better. Alternatively you could use a large wooden bird cage with 1.25 cm (½ in) chicken wire in front or a glass-sided aquarium with a wire or gauze lid.

The cage floor may be covered with sawdust, newspaper or even clean dry sand. Newspaper is recommended because, as well as being cheap to provide, the gerbils can tear it up to make a nest. Sand, however, enables the gerbils to burrow and, if you keep your pets in an aquarium tank and stack three or four large pieces of stone or slate to form an underground cave, you will be fascinated to watch your pets' activities.

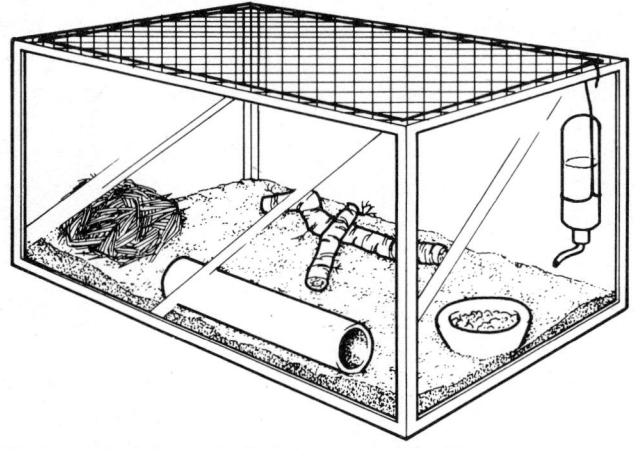

Figure 27 Aquarium furnished with sawdust, bedding material, water bottle, food bowl and playthings

Cleaning: Whichever type of floor covering you choose, do renew it every 2 or 3 weeks so that the cage is clean and sweet-smelling and ensure that hay or clean newspaper is always available as nesting material.

Accessories

You should provide your gerbils with a small, heavyweight food-bowl which cannot be knocked over and a water-bottle of the gravity type which can be fixed to the cage by means of an elastic band, a paper clip or a special suction pad. A water-bowl is not recommended for the gerbil as there is always the risk of these tiny creatures falling into the dish and drowning. You will discover that gerbils tend to drink less than other rodents but, nevertheless, fresh water should always be provided.

Figure 28 Agouti gerbil in bottom of cage with gnawing block and food and water bowls

Feeding

The diet of gerbils, jirds, jerboas and kangaroo rats is similar to that of the golden hamster and a good hamster mix, of the type sold in pet-shops, will provide a gerbil with the bulk of its requirements. This method of feeding entails less waste than others. A few small pieces of apple, carrot or green food should be added to provide vitamins and moisture. Alternatively you could provide a mixture of assorted nuts (especially peanuts), kibbled and flaked maize, wheat, sunflower seeds and spray millet. This also requires supplements in the form of occasional pieces of apple, greens, carrots or some other root vegetables. Some gerbils also enjoy titbits or raw meat and cheese and one or two live meal worms.

Unlike the hamster, the gerbil does not hoard its food so you will soon be able to work out how much to give each day as, if any food is left, you are obviously overfeeding. About 1 tablespoonful of food daily for each gerbil should be about right.

Health and commonsense care

Gerbils are hardy little animals and comparatively disease-free, but to keep them so they should not be offered a surfeit of food, particularly greens. Their average life-span in captivity is 3 years.

Handling

In handling a gerbil, the main problem is to prevent it from jumping out of your hands and becoming injured because it is so active. Hold your gerbil, over a table or near the floor, cupped in both hands and facing towards you. Do not hold it by the tail which is easily injured.

Gerbils handled regularly from weaning will scramble about on your shoulders and even an unfamiliar adult gerbil, if approached gently, is likely to show curiosity rather than fear at the sight of an outstretched human hand. But, I repeat, do not exhaust your gerbil, for exhaustion, particularly heat exhaustion, can result in death.

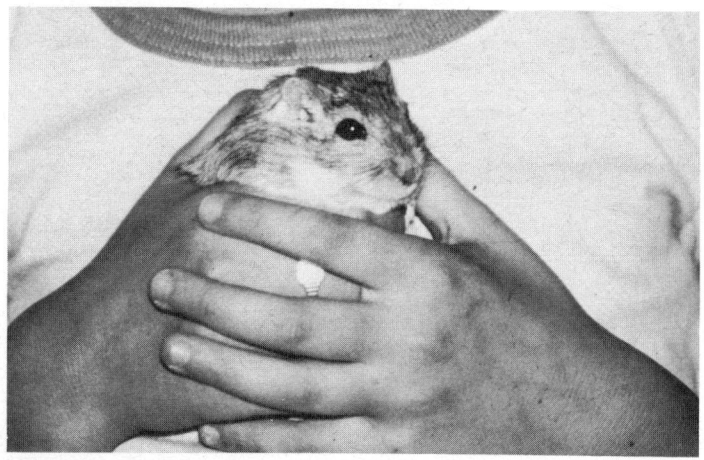

Figure 29   Handling your gerbil

Diseases

It is possible for a gerbil to have epileptic-type seizures, although there is some suggestion that this condition is an instinctive response to confuse predators.

Gerbils suffer from no known internal parasitic infection, but they can be host to a mange mite and this may require veterinary treatment. The most serious endemic gerbil disease is Tyzzer's disease, a liver condition, the symptoms of which are diarrhoea, general lethargy and tiredness with loss of appetite, wasting and collapse. This disease is usually fatal but is likely to occur only when a large number of gerbils are kept together.

Breeding

Mongolian gerbils, if kept in breeding pairs throughout their lives, can raise as many as nine litters together and often display an unmistakable affection for each other.

Sex determination
The male gerbil is usually heavier than the female. When sexing youngsters, you will notice that the distance between the anus and the genital slit is greater in the male.

Mating
Young gerbils can be paired and left together when they are about 6–10 weeks old. If you are introducing two strange adults, however, great care should be taken. For the first few days, they should be separated by a wire mesh until they appear to have struck up a friendship. They may then be released together but they should be watched carefully and separated if they begin to fight. Continue to put them together in this way until they become accustomed to each other. The female is ready for mating at 9–12 weeks of age and the male about 1 week later. The female comes into season every 4 or 5 days during a breeding life of about 17 months.

Pregnancy
It is difficult to tell when a female is pregnant but the young are born about 23 days after mating. A nesting box should be provided.

Birth
The average litter size is four, although litters of twelve have been recorded. Usually, it is safe to leave the male with the female as the male gerbil is a helpful caring father. You should resist any attempt to examine the nest as this may disturb the female, causing her to abandon or destroy her young.

Weaning
The babies open their eyes after about 21 days and are generally weaned, without outside assistance, at around 28 days. Since the female can mate again almost immediately after birth, a second litter may be born while the first litter is still being cared for. In this case, it is advisable to take the older babies away. If you pick them up, do so by holding the base of the tail as close as possible to the body.

As long as they remain immature, litter mates may remain in one cage. After 4 months, however, the males should be either moved to separate cages to prevent fighting or established with young females to form fresh breeding pairs.

Figure 30 Mother gerbil and young

The show world

The Fancy

In the UK, the National Mongolian Gerbil Society looks after the interests of gerbil owners of all ages, organises shows in London, the Midlands and the north-west of England and issues regular Newsletters and a Yearbook. The Club is active in developing new colours and gives a great deal of advice to members.

Gerbil classes are also being introduced into a number of general fanciers' club shows, membership of which could well prove worthwhile. There is not, as yet, a governing body for gerbils in the USA or in Canada and specific gerbil shows are not held there, although most of the colours obtainable in the UK are now available in the USA.

At the moment, gerbils in the USA are kept either for research or as pets. The National Mongolian Gerbil Society in the UK deals with quite a number of transatlantic enquiries.

It is probably true to say that the practise of exhibiting gerbils as show animals is still in its infancy. However, as appreciation of this tiny creature grows, no doubt more facilities will be provided. Meanwhile the National Mongolian Gerbil Society has fully accepted show standards for a number of colours and varieties (see Table 8) and provisional standards exist for Grey Agouti, Argente (Cream) and Patched varieties. Do not expect to find specimens such as these at your local pet-shop.

Table 8. Standardised colours and varieties of Mongolian gerbil

White-bellied Golden Agouti	Soft golden red top colour evenly covered with black ticking over the back and sides, carried down to dark grey at the roots. The belly fur to be as white as possible, clearly demarcated from the top colour and to be approximately half as wide as the ticked upper coat. A line of unticked golden hairs to run along the demarcation line and extend down the outside of the legs. The top of the tail only shall be the same as the body, ticked with black and with a ridge of long black hairs beginning near the root and ending in an almost black tuft. Black eyes, encircled with light grey hair, black toenails, black and white whiskers. Ears covered with light grey hair, bordered with soft golden red and free from ticking.
Argente (Golden)	Clear golden colour with no ticking or shading. White belly fur clearly demarcated from the top colour, approximately half the width of the top colour and just visible from the side. Golden hairs shall run down the outside of the legs. Blue-grey underfur throughout. Tail shall be golden throughout with a ridge of white hairs running along the upper surface from the root to form a tuft at the tip. Ruby eyes, white feet, neutral toenails, white whiskers. Ears edged with white hairs.

White Spot	Ground colour as for unspotted variety. There should be a spot on the nose, forehead and nape of the neck, all placed centrally and as round as possible, large and even in size with no hair of any other colour. There should be a tuft of white hairs at the tail tip. White feet, neutral toenails.
Pink-Eyed White	Pure white hair down to the skin with no shading or marking. Clear pink eyes, neutral toenails, white whiskers. Ears flesh-coloured covered with fine white hairs.
Black	Jet black hair down to the skin, even all over. Black eyes, toenails and whiskers. Ears covered with fine short black hairs.
Dove	Soft dove grey, as light as possible. Ruby eyes, neutral toenails, light grey whiskers. Ears covered with fine soft grey hair.

From information supplied by the National Mongolian Gerbil Society.

Breeding for show purposes

All I can do is repeat the sound advice to breed only from sound proven stock, from a true colour line and from animals which are first-class examples of the standard laid down for their breed or variety, with a winning record. While interbreeding is the method most likely to produce colour mutations, the process nearly always involves a risk of deformity so, in the case of the Mongolian gerbil, it has been abandoned in favour of selective breeding. Do all this and you may be lucky, but don't anticipate a litter of prospective champions — pets are just as easy to love and doubtless you will be able to find deserving homes for them.

5
Mice

Origins of the mouse

Mention the word 'mouse' to a great many people and the mere thought will induce an involuntary shudder. On the other hand, speak about fancy mice to a fancier and you will be bowled over immediately by their enthusiasm, friendliness and eagerness to acquaint you with the pleasures and scope of the hobby.

Fancy mice originate from the common House mouse, *Mus musculus,* the creature which has followed Man wherever he produces or stores food. Keep animal foods in a sack rather than a galvanised bin, or cake in a pantry out of its tin, and the determined mouse will nibble its way in.

Undoubtedly, the House mouse, for all its attractiveness, *is* a pest. Nevertheless, in common with the hamster and gerbil, its usefulness in the laboratory since the end of the last century is indisputable. In addition, its mutant forms are so attractive that, after more than 75 years of selective breeding, over forty different varieties of fancy mice are recognised in both the UK and the USA. (Surprisingly, fancy breeds were first exhibited in the seventeenth century in Japan!) The hobby has now become worldwide and the proverbial white mouse of schoolboy fame has been joined by many other attractive varieties.

Characteristics of the mouse

Mice are merry little animals belonging to the rodent family and make ideal pets, especially where there is limited room for pet-keeping. They are also very clean animals if properly cared for, quickly become tame and provide hours of entertainment for their owners. Easily tamed by hand-feeding and nocturnal by nature, pet mice will only bite if frightened.

Sadly mice rarely live for more than 18 months to 2 years, but if you can harden your heart to this, the fact that they are easy to keep and great fun to exhibit should, to some extent, make up for their short life span, especially when you can make their short lives extremely happy ones.

Figure 31 An Agouti mouse

Figure 32 One of the Marked varieties of mouse

Choosing and buying your mouse

The National Mouse Club (NMC) has used its authority wisely and accepted only those varieties which it has from time to time considered worthy of placing in the Club standards. There are so many standardised colours of fancy mice that the NMC has also found it necessary, for the sake of convenience, the divide the varieties into four groups: Self Colours, Tans, Marked and Any Other Variety (see Table 9).

Table 9. Standardised breeds of mouse

SELFS	Colour carried evenly throughout the whole body, extending to the skin, ears, nose, nails, tail, belly and the set-on of the tail. Recognised colours: Black (black eye), Blue (black eye), Champagne (pink eye), Chocolate (black eye), Cream (pink or black eye), Dove (pink eye), Fawn (pink eye), Red (black eye), Silver (pink or black eye), White (pink or black eye).
TANS	Any of the standard colours (except Red and White for genetical reasons) with a rich golden belly clearly demarcated along the flanks, chest and jaws. No brindling or guard hairs. Eye colour as in Selfs. Feet tan inside and top colour elsewhere.
MARKED	
Dutch	Evenly balanced patches on each side of the face, extending around the eyes and including the ears, but not running under the jaw. A saddle extending from the tail to the middle of the body, clean cut at the top and underneath. Stops on the hind feet to fall midway between toes and the hock. Markings may be of any recognised colour. Pink or black eye.

Evens	Of recognised colour with evenly balanced markings and free of runs. The more spots or patches, the better. Pink or black eye.
Brokens	Spots or patches well distributed all over the head and body, uniform in size and numerous. There must be a spot or patch on one side of the nose. As far removed from the Dutch and Even in pattern as possible. Pink or black eye.
Variegated	Any recognised colour, evenly splashed over and under the body and free from any spots or solid patches as found in Evens and Brokens. Pink or black eye.
Himalayan	White with coloured points, i.e. nose, feet, ears, tail. Black or red eye.
Chinchillas	Intermediate shade of pearl grey with slate-blue undercolour. Hairs tipped with black. Belly and inside of feet white. Black eye.
Astrex	Curly coat of any recognised colour. Curly whiskers.
Silver Fox	Black, blue or chocolate. White belly. White ticking on feet, sides and rump. Black eyes.
Seal Point Siamese	Medium beige body colour, shaded over saddles and hindquarters. Seal points on muzzle, ears, feet, tail and root.
Long-haired	Long silky coat of any recognised colour.
Rump White	Any recognised colour with a white rump, hind feet and tail. No white markings elsewhere.
Tricolour	With three contrasting patches of colour on the back and sides.

SATINS	A high-sheen coat of any recognised colour with a satin-like or metallic gloss.

ANY OTHER VARIETY

Agouti	Rich brown or golden with even dark or black ticking. Golden brown belly ticked as on top. Feet as body colour with ticking. Black eye.
Silver Agouti	As above but silvery grey.
Cinnamons	Rich golden tan with rich brown ticking. Black eye.
Sables	Rich dark brown on top, shading to a rich golden tan belly. Black eye.
Marten Sables	Rich dark sepia shading to paler colour on lower jaws, sides and flanks. White belly. Black eye.
Pearls	Palest silver shading to a whitish undercolour. Each hair tipped with grey or black. Black eye.
Argentes	Blend of light fawn and silver with blue undercolour. Golden fawn belly. Feet as top. Pink eye.
Argente Creme	Blend of deep cream and silver with pale blue undercolour. White belly. Feet as body. Pink eye.
Silver Grey, Brown or Fawn	Blue-black undercolour in Greys, bright orange in Fawns, deep chestnut in Browns. Silver carried on to feet. Black eyes except for Silver Fawns which may have pink eyes or black eyes. Silver Grey are recognised in three shades: dark, medium and light.

Obtaining pet mice could not be easier. It has been estimated, in theory, that a pair of mice can be responsible for the production of 30 000 offspring in one year, as does come into season every 4 or 5 days. Pet-shops almost always have mice available and they are often kept in schools under laboratory conditions. The exhibiting and breeding of mice has such a popular following, however, that it would be a pity to make a purchase without first getting to know a few breeders, seeing some of the varieties available and, if possible, attending a fanciers' show.

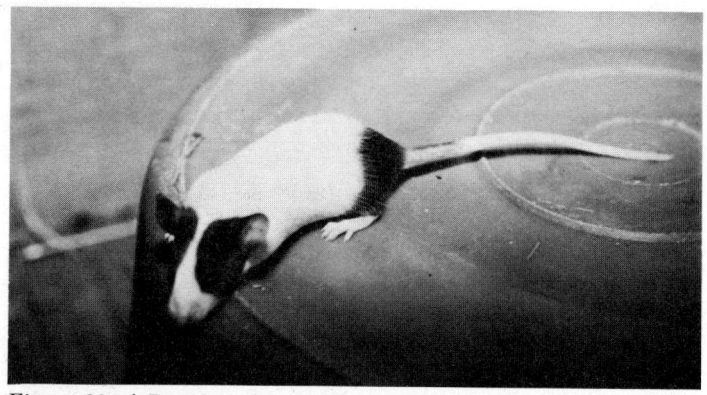

Figure 33   A Dutch mouse with typical markings

What you will need

Accommodation

A wooden cage with a glass front and a removable tray at the bottom, like those on sale in most pet-shops, is perfectly suitable. Alternatively, an all-glass aquarium with a ventilated lid provides a good home and is easy to keep clean. Mice can be kept singly or two females can be kept together if you do not want them to breed.

Whatever you choose, the cage should be furnished with a small nesting box, well above floor level, and a ladder for access. The inmates will make their own nest of wood shavings and small pieces of paper and these should be provided.

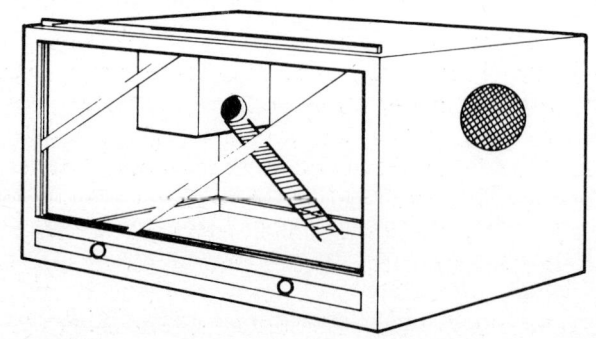

Figure 34   A typical wooden mouse cage with nest box

Cleaning: The bottom of the cage should be covered with a layer of sawdust, which should be changed at least twice a week, while the whole cage and nesting box should be thoroughly scrubbed out once a month with diluted disinfectant, every trace of which should be removed afterwards.

Accessories

A food bowl should be provided, sufficiently heavy not to be turned over, and also a water bottle of the gravity type.

Figure 35 A commercially available cage with accessories

Feeding

Mice have ferocious appetites and their diet should be mainly cereal in nature. A dry mixture can be prepared from rolled oats, breadcrumbs and mixed bird seed, to which a few drops of cod liver oil and a tiny pinch of table salt may be added. They should also be given a little green food or a small piece of carrot. Do not leave any uneaten food in the cage to become stale. Contrary to popular belief, cheese should not be given to tame mice, nor chocolate, as these items are liable to make the animals smell. Drinking water should always be available.

It is possible to get a prepared concentrated mouse food from pet-shops, where you should also be able to purchase sawdust. Items such as nuts, brown bread, greenstuff and even milk should also be offered and you may like to add treats in the form of young grass, dandelion, chickweed, cauliflower leaves and even a small dog biscuit.

Health and commonsense care

Handling
Naturally you will want to let your pet out of its cage for exercise and so that you may fondle it but every care should be taken to prevent it from escaping. Never hold a mouse by the tail without supporting its body in the palm of your hand and always hold it gently but sufficiently firmly to prevent it from getting loose.

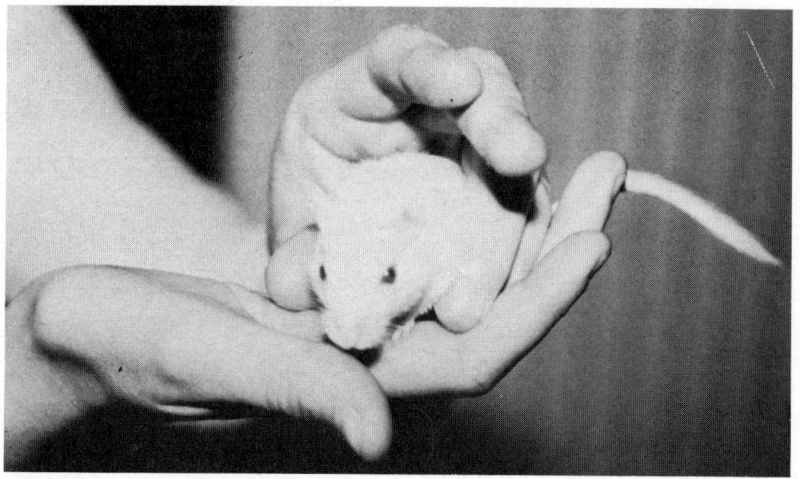

Figure 36   A White mouse showing correct handling

Diseases
In common with other rodents, provided that the mouse is kept under hygienic conditions, correctly fed and cleaned out properly, it is unlikely to contract any disease.

It is, however, important to observe your pet closely and to note any irregularities in behaviour. Some of the things to watch are: unnatural legarthy, discharge from the eyes or nose, an inclination of the head to one side (which might indicate an ear infection) and diarrhoea or constipation. Contact the veterinary surgeon within 24 hours if anything seems amiss.

Breeding

Sex determination
This becomes simpler after 10 days as the doe's teats become quite pronounced. If you examine the sex organs of the entire litter at this time and compare the differences, you will have little difficulty in distinguishing between the sexes by the time the next litter arrives.

Mating
The male should be ready for its first mating at 10 weeks and the female at 12 weeks. They should be placed together in a fairly small breeding box. The male should be removed as soon as the female is seen to be pregnant. Generally it is best to place him with other females as he is liable to lose condition if left alone too long.

Pregnancy
The gestation period is 19–21 days. If there are several pregnant does together, it is best to separate them before they have their litters.

Birth
Mice have litters of between four and eighteen babies. About 24 hours after a birth, you may very gently and carefully look into the nest, giving the mother a titbit to distract her attention. A quick glance will reveal any dead baby which should, of course, be removed. The young are born blind but, even when they are 2 days old, you will be able to see the pink or black colour of their eyes through the tiny, almost transparent lids. Their eyes open after 7 or 8 days. At first, their bodies are naked but, after a day or two, the hair will start to grow.

After the first inspection, the litter may be examined daily but the young mice should not be handled until they emerge from the nest.

Weaning
At 3–4 weeks, the young mice will be running about and feeding themselves. Give them a little oatmeal and keep a pot of bread and milk in the cage for them until they fully adjust to the adult diet. Feed them once a day, adjusting the quantity to suit. At 7 weeks, the does can be caged together.

The show world

The Fancy

It was in the UK, in the early 1890s, that a few fanciers started writing to the late lamented magazine *Fur and Feather*, asking if organisations might like to include a few mouse classes in their schedules. A number of people responded and the first reported class for mice was held at Oxford in 1892 and was won by a Mr William Wild, who exhibited a 'Cinnamon Red'. (Walter Maxey, however, a respected mouse expert, writing some time after, states that Wild's winner was, in fact, a Black.)

In any event, by 1893, the idea of exhibiting mice had caught on. The St Helens Show in Lancashire included three mouse classes in the schedule, which attracted great interest, while a cup was presented at Leicester and was won by a Mr Crompton of Birmingham with a Fawn (a Self Red). A class for mice was also included by the Abingdon Society in Berkshire and Mr Maxey succeeded in getting yet another in the schedule of a show in east London. Indeed, by 1895, it was clear that there was sufficient support to warrant a club and the National Mouse Club came into being.

It ought to be mentioned that, to their credit, a number of fanciers who served on that first committee, including a Mr Enoch Welburn and a Miss Grimston, were primarily cavy (guinea-pig) fanciers and it was they who helped to get the mouse Fancy off the ground. Indeed, in 1896, Mr Welburn, who was Secretary of the Cavy (Guinea-Pig) Club, decided that he could not handle both jobs so the latter responsibility was passed to Walter Maxey, who had originally turned down the post because he felt he was too young. Mr Maxey was National Mouse Club Secretary from 1897 to 1906. He designed the Maxey show cage and, in 1897, organised the first mouse-only show, which was held at Stratford in east London, when the best in show was taken by George Barber, exhibiting what was described as a 'Tricoloured' but, in fact, was a heavily marked Brown Sable!

In the 1950/60s, there was a fancy mouse society in the USA which unfortunately died out. The International Mouse Society, however, which is based in Wisconsin, USA, is still in existence.

Registration

The National Mouse Club (NMC) is the parent body of the various specialist clubs throughout the UK. It is the NMC which draws up exhibitors' rules and also the standards by which mice are judged. It arranges its own important shows and has a long list of valuable cups, including the Mendel gold cup for best type, which it offers at specified shows.

One of the main objects of the NMC is to promote the breeding and exhibiting of fancy mice, to publish the definition of the true type as the only recognised and unvarying standard by which fancy mice shall be judged and to adopt standards relating to the several varieties. It is, therefore, in the interest of every fancier to join the NMC, thereby receiving a Year Book, a Rule Book and a Standard Book, the names and addresses of all other members and much other useful information. The Year Book contains show dates, advertisements of mice for sale and also breeding and showing equipment. If you wish to set up your own mouse club and/or to register a prefix or affix, you may do so upon application to the Hon. Secretary, together with a nominal fee.

Specialist clubs

There are in the UK, quite a number of area mouse clubs affiliated to the NMC, including the Airedale Mouse Club and the Calder Valley Mouse Club in west Yorkshire, the London and Southern Counties Mouse Club, and the Midlands Mouse Club (which is based in Atherstone, Warwickshire); others are listed on p. 106. All these clubs hold shows at which mice are judged according to NMC standards. Membership will enable the fancier to be informed of club shows within reasonable travelling distance, where mice classes are to be included.

Overseas readers should write to the International Mouse Club for information of this type, remembering to include return postage or an International Reply Coupon with each enquiry.

There do not appear to be any clubs specialising in particular colours but, no doubt, with the growing popularity of the hobby, this is something we can look forward to in the future.

Exhibiting

When entering mice for a NMC-sponsored show, certain procedures should be observed.

Shows are, as a rule, advertised beforehand in newsletters. Many show promoters, including secretaries of local mouse clubs, send out schedules automatically to known exhibitors so, if your name is not already on their list, they will be only too pleased to include it.

It is the duty of the exhibitor to read the advertisement or schedule carefully and to follow any instructions given. Entries should be made as early as possible. This is helpful to the show secretary and ensures that the necessary labels and other information reaches you in plenty of time. If no entry form is supplied, entries can be made out on plain paper as follows:

Class No:.......... Variety:............	Also in classes:.........	Fees: ....
Name...	No. of Exhibits	....
Address	No. of Rail Labels required	....
....	No. of Entries	....

There is a small fee for each entry in each class and the total amount must be enclosed with the entry form.

If you are despatching your mouse to a show by rail, enough dry food should be included to last until the exhibit arrives safely back home. Mice are fed after judging but a little extra is a good precaution. It is advisable to despatch stock early in the morning prior to the day of the show, unless the venue is fairly near, in which case the despatch may be left until rather later in the day. You should aim at your stock reaching the destination town the night before the show. Travelling exhibits are returned immediately after a show and should be collected from the home station late the same day or early next morning.

It is a rule that, at all shows held under NMC patronage, mice must be exhibited in standard Maxey show cages, coloured green outside and red inside. The standard colours are the shades usually known as Middle Brunswick Green and Royal (Signal) red. Only one mouse can be exhibited per cage.

It is often possible to buy such cages through advertisements in club newsletters or from other club members. However, many people make their own cages from specifications supplied by the mouse clubs.

The London and Southern Counties Club makes a point of mentioning in its handbook that exhibitors should not worry if they do not have their own cages, as the Club owns a number of show pens which may be hired at their shows, free of charge and without prior application. It must be emphasised, however, that this facility applies to the Club's own table shows and not to the open shows held at various southern towns during July, August and September at which mouse classes are included.

Although mention has been made of despatching mice to far-off destinations, in the case of an exhibition round the corner, exhibitors will doubtless wish to transport their exhibits themselves, albeit properly labelled, to arrive at the centre at the designated time.

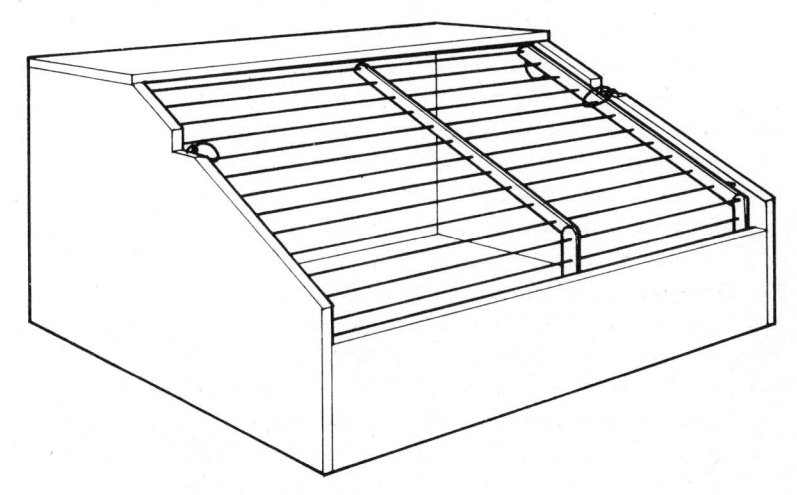

Figure 37   A Maxey show cage

Judging

Judges for table shows are selected from a club's panel of judges who will adjudicate in accordance with the standards laid down by the National Mouse Club. These are usually people who have had many years experience in the Fancy and considerable experience in exhibiting and breeding.

The mice are judged according to a general standard of excellence adopted by the National Mouse Club. This states that:

> 'The Mouse must be long in the body, with long, clean head, not too fine or pointed at the nose; the eyes should be large, bold and prominent; the ears large and tulip shaped, free from creases, carried erect with plenty of width between them. The body should be long and slim, a trifle arched over the loin, and racy in appearance; the tail, which must be free from kinks, should come well out of the back, and be thick at the root or set-on, gradually tapering like a whip lash to a fine end, the length being about equal to that of the mouse's body. The coat

should be short, perfectly smooth, glossy and sleek to the hand. The mouse should be perfectly tractable and free from any vice and not subject to fits or other similar ailments. A Mouse absent of whiskers, blind in one or both eyes, carrying external parasites, having a tumour, sore or patches of fur missing, suffering from any obvious disease or deformity or kinked tails shall be disqualified.'

General remarks are added to the effect that written standards are necessarily under some handicap. Words cannot convey an exact idea of what any mouse should look like and this applies particularly to any definition of colour.

In judging, which calls for a keen eye and usually many years of experience, adjudication is based on a points system; the perfect specimen merits 100 points. A standard of points is laid down for all the varieties so that they may receive so many points e.g. for perfect nose marking, ear marking, hair markings, size, condition, tail. An unstandardised mouse is not eligible for a Championship.

A mouse can be made a Champion. However, it must be a very fine mouse which has won five first prizes, awarded at not less than three NMC supported shows. Also, the first prizes must have been won in a straight class, Section Challenge or Best of Section comprising, at the time of the judging, not less than seven exhibits, belonging to no fewer than three exhibitors, actually on the table at the time of judging. If there are less than seven exhibits in the class, they must belong to at least five exhibitors. A mouse winning a first prize in a qualifying Section Challenge shall be deemed to have automatically gained a point in previously winning its straight class at that show. A mouse winning Best in Show or Best Opposite Age shall be awarded an extra point towards a Championship. All Cup Shows (five of which take place in the UK each year) are designated as Championship events and first prize winners in straight classes are allowed Championship points irrespective of entry and exhibitor requirements.

For Single, Double, Treble etc Championship, the number of first prizes necessary is in multiples of five, i.e. ten for a Double and so on. A mouse gaining five Championships shall be designated Supreme Challenge.

Types of shows and classes

As by now you will have realised, the procedure at fanciers' shows is for an event to be termed either a pen or a table show. At a pen show, the judge comes round and examines the exhibits in their cages whereas at the more common table show, the exhibits are shown to the judge or judges, on the judging table.

An example of the range of classes available in a typical table show can be seen in Table 10.

Table 10. Classes featuring in a typical mouse show schedule

Self	Any Other Variety
Pink-eyed White	Agouti/Cinnamon
Black/Blue	Argente/Argente Creme
Champagne/Fawn	Silvered/Pearl
Cream	Any Other Variety
Any Other Colour	CHALLENGE
CHALLENGE	
	Stud buck
Tan	Doe
Black/Chocolate	GRAND CHALLENGE
Champagne/Silver	
Any Other Colour	SUPREME CHALLENGE
CHALLENGE	
	Supporters
Marked	Juvenile/Novice
Dutch/Rumpwhite	Unstandardised/Pet
Broken/Himalayan	
Any Other Colour	
CHALLENGE	Best in Show
Satin	Best Opposite Age
Self	
Tan	
Any Other Colour	
CHALLENGE	

Each class is divided into adult and juvenile.
Information taken from the results of the London and Southern Counties Mouse Club Table Show, December 1980.

Breeding for show purposes
Obviously the aim is to produce a champion mouse of a chosen variety but, as with all stock, it is unlikely that a superb specimen will result as the offspring of inferior parents and straining for

perfection will bring desired results only where one has acquired sound foundation stock, through experience and obtaining the advice of seasoned fanciers.

Records of breeding operations and results should always be kept so that a wise selection can be made for future pairings. A plan put forward by the NMC is to attach to each doe's box a card with information as to the number or name of the doe, date of birth, colour, sire's number, dam's and buck's numbers and the date and size of the litter when born.

In the case of the buck's box, the card can bear the buck's number, date of birth, colour, sire's and dam's numbers. These cards may be moved with the mice and, if eventually they are filed, complete records are at hand for reference at any time. Indeed, as the NMC point out, if the fancier is so-minded, he may add to his pleasure and education by using his mouse-breeding as a means of studying genetics and the general laws of heredity which is a fascinating occupation.

6
Rats

Origins of the rat

The fancy rat, like the fancy mouse, has wild ancestors — in this case the Norway rat (*Rattus norvegicus*) — and the tame variety has been acquired through selective breeding in laboratories. The wild rat has always been disliked and even feared, because of its association with disease, an association sometimes unfairly ascribed to the tame variety, which has developed into a most attractive and amenable pet, well-suited to captivity.

Characteristics of the rat

The rat, like the mouse, is a rodent of the family Muridae. Both species have the same sharp muzzle, a long tail almost half the length of the body, which acts as a balancing aid when climbing, and rootless, continuously-growing incisors; both can eat with their fore paws.

Perhaps surprisingly, rats like people and it has been suggested that human companionship may compensate, to some extent, for the loneliness of a solitary pet rat. Nevertheless, although rats can live on their own, they are best kept in single-sex pairs. Strangely, in this instance, males are more amenable than females and, provided that they have never been in the company of a female, will almost always live happily together.

Rats are intelligent, gentle, affectionate and seldom if ever bite. They are easily tamed if hand-fed and will supply lots of amusement running around an exercise wheel. A word of caution; be careful that their long tails do not get caught. The rat's lifespan is longer than that of the mouse — over 2 years — and they are in prime exhibition condition during their first year.

Figure 38 An Agouti rat

Choosing and buying your rat

There are a number of varieties of rat from which to choose as rats are now bred in many different colours and patterns (see Table 11). There is even a Rex variety.

If you want a rat that you can enter in competitions, you should choose one of good size with a long, racy body arched over the hindquarters. It should be firmly fleshed with a clean long head, not too pointed at the nose, and the ears should be of a fair size, tulip-shaped and set well apart. The coat should be glossy, sleek and soft but not too long. The tail should be as long as the head and body combined, thick at the base and tapering to a fine point. Ears, feet and tail should be covered with fine hair. The buck is larger than the doe and has a harsher coat. Poor condition or health, bald areas, scaliness of the ears, or a short or kinked tail are serious faults in a show animal and lack of whiskers will result in automatic disqualification.

Figure 39 A White rat

Table 11. Varieties of rat and their judging requirements

COLOUR	
Agouti	Rich ruddy brown, evenly ticked with black guard hairs. Dark grey to black base fur. Silvery grey belly. Black eyes.
Cinnamon	Warm russet brown, evenly ticked with chocolate guard hairs. Mid-grey base fur. Belly as for the Agouti but lighter. Black eyes.
Silver Fawn	Rich orange fawn, evenly ticked with silver guard hairs. White belly, clearly defined with no irregularities or brindling. Red eyes.

Pearl	Palest silver shading to creamish undercolour. Each hair to be tipped with grey evenly over the entire animal. Pale silver grey belly. Black eyes.
Cinnamon Pearl	Coat to consist of three bands of colour — cream, blue, orange — with silver guard hairs to give an overall golden appearance with a silver sheen. Pale silver grey belly. Black eyes.
Black	Deep solid black devoid of dinginess, white hairs or patches. Black base fur. Black eyes.
Mink	Even mid grey brown devoid of dinginess, silvering or patches and having a bluish sheen. Black eyes.
Champagne	Evenly warm beige with no suggestion of dullness or greyness. Red eyes.
Pink-Eyed White	As white as possible, devoid of creamy tinge or staining. Pink eyes.
Siamese	Medium beige body colour shading gradually and evenly over the saddle and hindquarters towards the belly, being darkest at the base of the tail. Tail colour to extend for the length of the tail. Light beige belly. Rich dark sepia points shading evenly into the body colour. Ruby eyes.
Himalayan	White body colour, free from stains and even throughout. Rich dark sepia points — as dark as possible. Red eyes. N.B. Colour should not extend upwards from the eyes, downwards from the ears, beyond the elbows or the fore-legs and the ankles on the hind legs, or more than halfway up the rump from the tail. Feet should be solid colour throughout.

PATTERN

Hooded — Pure white body devoid of yellowish tinge or staining with coloured hood covering the head, throat and shoulders and continuous with the saddle down the spine to the tail. The saddle should be 63–127 cm (¼–½ in) wide, even and unbroken. The edges of the hood and saddle should be clear cut with no brindling.

Berkshire — The body colour shall be of a recognised colour variety. The markings should be symmetrical with as much white on the chest and belly as possible but not extending up the sides of the body. The edges shall be clear cut with no brindling. A white spot on the forehead is desirable. The hind feet should be white to the ankle and the fore legs and tail to half their length.

Irish — Body colour shall conform to a recognised colour variety. There should be a white equilateral triangle on the chest, of good size, clear, devoid of brindling and not extending in a streak down the belly but occupying all the space between the forelegs. The fore-feet should be white and the hind feet white to half their length.

Capped — The colour should follow the line of the lower jaw bone and not extend past the ears or under the chin. There should be a white blaze or spot on the face and the rest of the body should be white. Colour to conform to a recognised colour variety. White to be pure and devoid of staining.

Variegated — The head and shoulders to be of any distinct colour with a white blaze on the forehead. The variegation to cover the body from the shoulders to the tail, including the sides. Belly colour to be white, devoid of creamy tinge or staining. Colour to conform to any recognised colour variety.

Silvered	The coat to be of a recognised colour, containing equal numbers of silvered and non-silvered hairs. Each silvered hair should have as much of its length white as possible; a coloured tip allowed. Silvering to give an overall sparkling appearance. It should not be possible to confuse a Silver with a Pearl or a Self.
COAT *Rex*	The coat to be evenly dense and not excessively harsh, with as few guard hairs as possible. Coat to be evenly curled; to a lesser extent on the belly. Curly vibrissae are normal for a Rex. Colour to conform to a recognised colour or pattern variety.

From information supplied by the National Fancy Rat Society

Your local pet dealer will probably be able to offer a pet rat or, at any rate, to introduce you to fellow-fanciers. In any event, if you contact the National Fancy Rat Society, they will do all they possibly can to help you.

What you will need

Accommodation

Rats, like mice, are gnawers and will try to escape if they can and so cages made of softwood will never contain them. A larger version of the mouse-cage — single storey with a raised gallery — is suitable for a rat and two rats can be housed comfortably in a cage 45 cm (18 in) high with a floor area of 75 × 50 cm (30 × 20 in) with a mesh lid. Aquaria can also be used and are easier to clean. Hay, wood-shavings or shredded paper (not newspaper) may be used as bedding, with a floor-covering of sawdust. Separate sleeping quarters are not necessary.

Both rats and mice are best kept at temperatures between 20° and 25°C (68° and 77°F), and although they can survive lower temperatures, it is not advisable, particularly in the UK, to keep them out of doors.

Figure 40 A typical commercially available all-metal cage with food and water bowls

Cleaning: Rats are quite clean animals and, if kept in pairs, will spend a considerable amount of time grooming each other. They will not smell if you remember to renew their floor-covering twice a week, allowing the cage to dry thoroughly before replacing the litter. It is a good idea to return some of the old bedding which will retain some of the animals' scent. If your rats have magpie tendencies, when you have cleaned the cage you can return any items which are not likely to deteriorate.

Accessories
Water-bottles of the gravity type fixed to the outside of the cage are recommended. Rats are prodigious drinkers and you may find that two such bottles are necessary. A feeder of the hopper-type, obtainable from most pet-shops, is preferable to dishes, which will tend to become fouled.

Provision should be made for tunnelling as well as climbing. Lengths of piping will serve as substitute burrows. A gnawing block is essential.

Feeding

It is usual to provide rats in captivity with two meals a day. Specially prepared pellets can be obtained from pet-shops but you will find that these, even if supplemented with vegetable matter, will aggravate your pets' thirst.

A more varied diet is to be recommended, based on grain, such as barley, maize and rolled oats, together with either stale wholemeal bread, soaked in warm water and squeezed out, or dog meal. Mixed corn and limited amounts of sunflower seeds, together with carrot, complete a balanced diet. Fresh greenstuff, fruit, eggs, peanuts and milk are valuable supplements, especially for pregnant and nursing females who need an enriched diet and should be fed plenty of bread and milk. Water should be available at all times.

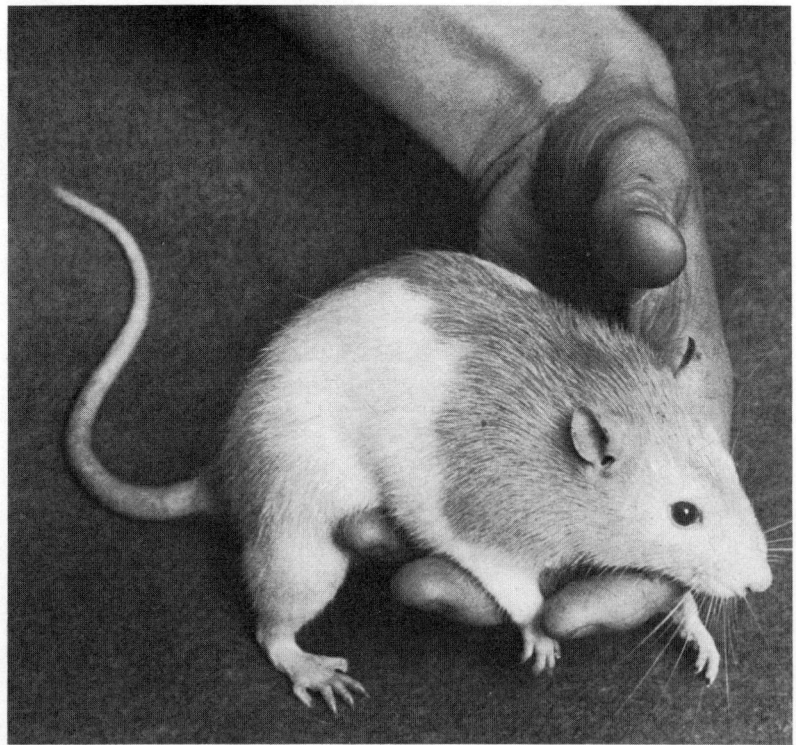

Figure 41 A Silver Fawn Hooded rat, showing the correct way of lifting

Health and commonsense care

Handling
Hold your rat in both hands or, if it is particularly docile, lift it by placing one hand over its back with its head held between your thumb and forefinger. You can then grip its tummy with your free fingers.

Diseases
Rats are very rarely ill if kept in clean surroundings with plenty of ventilation and an adequate diet. Overgrown incisors can be a problem but it is one which should not arise if adequate gnawing facilities are provided. Occasionally, in the winter, rats may show signs of having a 'cold' but this generally lasts only a few days. If this becomes more severe, veterinary assistance should be sought.

Breeding

Sex determination
It is difficult to distinguish between the sexes in young rats. The distance between the anus and the genital area is greater in the male than in the female but this is not easy to judge. In rats over 1 month old, however, a rudimentary scrotum should be discernible on the male.

Pairing
Rats are fully mature when 60 days old but ideally they should be between 3 and 10 months before breeding. One buck rat can be mated with up to ten does.

Pregnancy
The gestation period is approximately 22½ days and the does should be disturbed as little as possible during pregnancy. Ideally they should be segregated as soon as they are seen to be pregnant as, although the buck usually makes an excellent father, re-mating takes place immediately after the litter is born.

Birth
Litters are large, usually between six and twelve, but sometimes as many as twenty. The young are born blind, deaf and hairless. Their eyes open at about 14 days at which time they can begin to take solid food.

Weaning

They should be completely weaned by the age of 1 month and, at 4—5 weeks old, they should be removed. At 6 weeks, they should be kept in single sex groups.

The show world

The Fancy

The rat Fancy is a relatively new hobby, the National Fancy Rat Society (NFRS) having been formed as recently as 1976. According to Les Suttling, the Society's current helpful chairman, some rat and mouse clubs came into existence in the late 1800s and continued until 1914, at which time the rat side of the Fancy was discontinued due to lack of support. Luckily, this sorry state of affairs has been remedied and the NFRS is growing steadily, claiming members from all walks of life.

Rats do not have the same serious following in the USA, but the British Society has members there, as well as in Holland. The Dutch are great fanciers. The Society has made exciting progress since its formation; at that time there were mainly Pink-Eyed White, Silver Fawn and Black Hooded rats. New varieties are introduced from time to time. Prospective members should bear in mind that some varieties are extremely rare. Therefore, the Society needs breeders who are interested in producing new varieties and improving existing ones, as well as pet-keepers, who are the vanguard of the Society in establishing the rat as the 'superpet' (the Society's words) which it is.

Nationally, members are kept in touch through the NFRS journal, *Pro-Rat-A,* which is sent to members six times a year. The Society is most helpful in answering problems on pet rats, as long as a stamped addressed envelope is enclosed.

Specialist clubs

If there is no club dealing specifically with rats in your area, membership of a local general fanciers' club is to be recommended.

Exhibiting

In the UK, the NFRS holds monthly shows at venues such as Bradford, Blackburn, Portsmouth, Harlow, Surbiton, Richmond, Dagenham, Dartford and Peckham. The main show of the year is the London Championship Show, which is held every autumn. This is the biggest fur and feather show and exhibition in the UK and includes an award for the children's superpet of the year, which was won by a rat in 1980.

The London and Southern Counties Mouse Club holds classes at its shows for members with rats and exhibitors are able to hire special rat show pens. It is felt, however, that most intending rat exhibitors would prefer to obtain plastic aquaria which are the standard show cases of the NFRS and in which the majority of rats at table shows are exhibited. The standard judging requirements for the various rat varieties, as laid down by the NFRS, are listed in Table 11.

Useful addresses

General

United Kingdom
British Veterinary Association, 7 Mansfield Street, London W1M 0AT.
London Championship Show (all small caged pets) (Sec: Mrs Pat Gaskin), Chattisham, Ipswich, Suffolk IP8 3PE.
People's Dispensary for Sick Animals, PDSA House, Dorking, Surrey RH4 2LB.
Royal Society for the Prevention of Cruelty to Animals, Causeway, Horsham, Sussex RH12 1HG.
Southern Young Fanciers (Sec: Mr R. Chatfield), 27 Newton Road, Isleworth TW7 6QD.
Zoological Society of London, Regent's Park, London NW1.

United States of America
American Humane Association, 9725 East Hampden, Denver, Colorado 80231.
American and Plant Health Inspection Service, USDA, Room 703, Federal Building, 6505 Belcrest Road, Hyattsville, MD 20782.
American Society for the Prevention of Cruelty to Animals (ASPCA), 441 East 92nd Street, New York, NY 10028.
Office of Information, US Department of Agriculture, Washington 25, DC.

Rabbits

United Kingdom

Alaska Club: Ms Jenny Worker, 6 Adelaide Place, Ryde, Isle of Wight.

Angora Rabbits: Mr R. J. Whitcombe, 14 Alpine Road, Paulton, Avon BS18 5SD.

British Rabbit Council, Purefoy House, 7 Kirkgate, Newark, Nottingham.

Commercial Rabbit Association, CRA (FF), Tying House, Shurdington, Cheltenham GL51 5XF.

Greater London Lop Association: Mrs Taylor, 27 Ridley Road, Enfield, Middlesex.

National English Lop Club: Mrs P. J. Chapman, Dunvegan, Coombe Road, Southminster, Essex.

National Otter Rex Rabbit Club: Diane and Graham Dorward, 4 Belmont Road, Malvern WR14 1PL.

United States of America

American Rabbit Breeders Association, 4323 Murray Avenue, Pittsburg 16, Pennsylvania.

Guinea-pigs (Cavies)

United Kingdom

Cavy World, 20 Wesley Street, Farsley, Pudsey, LS28 5LE.

Crested Cavy Club: Mrs J. L. Pickering, Fernhill Cottage, Rouncil Lane, Kenilworth CV8 1NN.

Dalmatian and Roan Cavy Club: F. C. Holmes, Mid Farm Cottage, Harrold, Bedfordshire.

English Self Cavy Club: Mr A. J. Cooke, 1 Longridge Road, Woodthorpe, Nottingham.

Leslie Stud: Allen and Pauline Bone, 44 Canberra Gardens, Dagenham, Essex.

National Cavy Club: Mr. P. Parkinson, 23 Union Street, Slaithwaite, Yorkshire HD7 5ED

Peruvian Cavy Club: Mrs I. Turner, 1 Archdale Street, Syston, Leicestershire.

Southern Cavy Club: Mr and Mrs C. Clouter, 56 Allison Road, Bristol BS4 4PN.

Worthing Cavy Club: P. Francis, 177 King Edward Avenue, Worthing, Sussex.

United States of America
American Cavy Breeders Association: Mr G. L. Missler, 537 Tecumseh Street, Dundee, Michigan 48131.

Canada
Ontario Cavy Club Inc., Mrs A. Meade, R.R.I., Jarvis, Ontario N0A 1J0.

Hamsters

United Kingdom
Midland Hamster Club: Mrs W. Stokes-Clare, 3 Allied Close, Holbrooks, Coventry CV6 6GN.
National Hamster Council: Mr C. Lazenby, 14 Duke Street, Wigan, Greater Manchester.
Parslow's Hamster Farm, Common Side, Great Bookham, Leatherhead, Surrey.
Rotastak Hamster Club, 2 Finway, Dallow Road, Luton, Bedfordshire.
Southern Hamster Club: Mr D. Homes, 3 Peterborough Road, Leyton, London E10 6D11.
Yorkshire Hamster Club: Mr R. Hughes, 86 Sackville Road, Heaton, Newcastle-upon-Tyne NE6 5TB.

Gerbils

United Kingdom
National Mongolian Gerbil Society: Mrs M. Brookes, 3 Tracks Lane, Billinge, Wigan WN5 7BL.

Mice

United Kingdom
Airedale Mouse Club: Mr John Kellett, 56 Claremont Grove, Wrose, Shipley, West Yorkshire.
Calder Valley Mouse Club: Mr E. Longbottom, 109 Hopwood Lane, Halifax, West Yorkshire.

Greater Manchester Mouse Club: Mr Derek Taylor, 252 Stockport Road, Rose Hill, Marple, Cheshire.
London and Southern Counties Mouse Club: Mr Eric Jukes, 26 Downs Road, Enfield, Middlesex.
National Mouse Club: Mr Dennis Capstick, 7 Poplar Drive, Windhill, Shipley, West Yorkshire.
North Yorkshire Mouse Club: Mr and Mrs Horne, 2 Airy Hill, Filey, North Yorkshire.

United States of America
International Mouse Society: Gerald Franklyn Wright, 1419 Princeton Street, PO Box 64, Altoona, Wisconsin 54720.

Rats

United Kingdom
National Fancy Rat Society: Mr G. Izzard, 49 Grove Road, Surbiton, Surrey.

References

General

Bell, F. R. (19--) *Green Foods for Rabbits and Cavies* Eighth edition. Fancier's Library, Watmoughs Ltd, Bradford, Yorkshire.

Robinson, D. (1979) *Exhibition and Pet Hamsters and Gerbils* Spur Publications, Liss.

Smith, K. W. (1976) *Hamsters and Gerbils* Pet Care Guides, Bartholomew.

Smith, K. W. (1976) *Rats and Mice* Pet Care Guides, Bartholomew.

Rabbits

Brown, M. (1978) *Exhibition and Pet Rabbits* Spur Publications, Liss.

Dyson, H. (1970) *Rabbits* Pet and Fancy Series, Cassell, London.

Portsmouth, J. (1979) *Commercial Rabbit Meat Production* Saiga, Horsham.

Guinea-pigs

Sole, A. (1975) *Cavies* Second edition, Pet and Fancy Series, Cassell, London.

Turner, I. (1981) *Exhibition and Pet Cavies* Saiga, Horsham.

Hamsters

Parslow, P. (1979) *Hamsters* T.F.H. Publications, New Jersey.

Robinson, R. (1973) *The Right Way to Keep Hamsters* Paperfront Series, Eliot Right Way.

Snow, C. F. (1980) *Hamsters* Foyle, London.

Gerbils
Monroe, (1967) *Gerbils in Colour* T.F.H. Publications, New Jersey.
Schneider (1979) *Enjoy Your Gerbils* Pet Library.

Mice
Cooke, T. (1977) *Exhibition and Pet Mice* Spur Publications, Liss.
Jones, T. (ed.) (1980) *Encyclopedia of Pet Mice* T.F.H. Publications, New Jersey.

Rats
Richards, H. (19--) *Rats as Pets* T. F. H. Publications, New Jersey.

Index

Numbers in *italics* refer to illustrations.

Abyssinian guinea-pig 9, *37*, 38, 39-40, 47, 48
Accommodation for
 gerbils 69-70, *70*, 71, 73;
 guinea-pigs 9, 40-1, 45;
 hamsters 9, 53, 55-6, *56*, 57, *57*, 62;
 mice 10, 82, *89*;
 rabbits 8, *18*, 18-19, 26, 28, *29*;
 rats 10, 93, 98, *99*, 102-6
Agouti gerbil *71*;
 mouse *78*;
 rat *94*
Accessories for
 gerbils 70-1;
 guinea-pigs 43;
 hamsters 57, *57*;
 mice 83;
 rabbits 19-20;
 rats 99
American Cavy Breeders Association 40, 46, 47
American Rabbit Breeders Association Inc. 15, 27
Angora rabbit 28, *29*, 33

Birth of
 gerbils 73;
 guinea-pigs 46;
 hamsters 62-3;
 mice 85;
 rabbits 26;
 rats 101
Branches 19, 35
Breeding (*see also* Stock-breeding)
 gerbils 9, 72-4, *74*;
 guinea-pigs 36, 44-6, 51;
 hamsters 9, 61-3, 66;
 mice 85;
 rabbits 23-6, 34;
 rats 101
Breeds of
 gerbils 69, 70-1;
 guinea-pigs 38-40;
 hamsters 53, 54;
 mice 77, 79-81;
 rabbits 16-17, 27;
 rats 95-8, 102
British Rabbit Council 15, 27
Buying
 guinea-pigs 36-40;
 hamsters 54-5;
 mice 81-2;
 rabbits 13-18;
 rats 98

Californian rabbit 16-17, 27
Cavy *see* Guinea-pig
Characteristics of
 gerbils 68;
 guinea-pigs 35-6;
 hamsters 53-4;
 mice 77-8;
 rabbits 12-13;
 rats 93-4
Chinchilla rabbit 16, 27, 28
Chinese hamster 52, 53, 54
Choice of
 gerbils 68-9;
 guinea-pigs 36-40;
 hamsters 54-5;
 mice 79-81;
 rabbits 13-18;
 rats 94-8
Cleaning accommodation 7;
 gerbils 70;
 guinea-pigs 41;

INDEX

Cleaning accommodation of *(cont)*
  mice 83;
  rabbits 19, 20;
  rats 98
Cleaning utensils 20, 41
Cream hamster *63*

Dalmatian and Roan Cavy Club 46
Diet for
  gerbils 71;
  guinea-pigs 42, 45, 46;
  hamsters 58-9, 62, 63;
  mice 83, 85;
  rabbits 21, 26;
  rats 99-100
Diseases of
  gerbils 72;
  guinea-pigs 44;
  hamsters 60-1;
  mice 84;
  rabbits 22-3;
  rats 101
Djungarian hamster 52
Dutch
  guinea-pig 39, 40;
  mouse 79, *82*;
  rabbit 17, 27, 40

English guinea-pig 9, 38, 39-40, 47, 48;
  Chocolate Self *37*
English rabbit *14,* 17
English Self Cavy Club 46
European hamster 53, 54-5
Exhibiting 8, 10;
  gerbils 75;
  guinea-pigs 47-8;
  mice 87-9;
  rabbits 28;
  rats 102-3
Exhibition accommodation for
  mice *89*;
  rabbits 28, *29*;
  rats 102-6

Fancy,
  gerbil 69, 74-5;
  guinea-pig 40;
  hamster 63-4;
  mice 86;
  rabbit 14, 26-7;
  rat 102
Feeding 7;
  gerbils 68;
  guinea-pigs 9, 41-3;
  hamsters 58-9;
  mice 83-4;
  rabbits 10, 11-12, 20-2;
  rats 99-100
Flemish Giant rabbit 8, *8,* 27

Food containers 19-20, 22, 57, 70, 83, 99
Fur and Feather 15, 86

Gerbils 7, 67-76
Golden (Syrian) hamster 52-3, 54, *59*
Grooming
  guinea-pigs 38, 41, 47, *47,* 48;
  hamster *65*;
  rabbits 28
Grooming equipment for
  guinea-pigs 38;
  rabbits 20, 28
Guinea-pigs 9, 10, 35-51

Hamsters 7, 9, 10, 52-66
Handling
  gerbils, 9, 72, *72*;
  guinea-pigs 36;
  hamsters 9, *59,* 59-60;
  mice 84;
  rabbits 12, 22;
  rats 100, *100*;
Havana rabbit 16, 27
Health and care of
  gerbils 71-2;
  guinea-pigs 43-4;
  hamsters 54, 59-61;
  mice 84;
  rabbits 22-4;
  rats 100-1
Heat exhaustion 10, 40, 68, 72
Hibernation 54
Himalayan
  guinea-pig 39, 40;
  hamster *58*;
  rabbit *15,* 17
Hooded rat, Silver Fawn *100*

Injuries 9, 60
International Mouse Society 86, 87

Judging
  guinea-pigs 48, 49, *49*;
  hamsters 64;
  mice 89-90;
  rabbits 30;
  rats 103

Libyan gerbil 68, 69
Lifespan of
  gerbils 9, 71;
  guinea-pigs 9;
  hamsters 9, 53;
  mice 78;
  rabbits 8;
  rats 94
Long-haired hamster *65*
Lop rabbit 17, 24, *25*;
  Blue *14*

INDEX

Marked mouse 78, 79
Mating
 gerbils 73;
 guinea-pigs 45;
 hamsters 53, 62;
 mice 85;
 rabbits 24;
 rats 101
Mice 10, 77-92
Mongolian gerbil 67, 68, 69, 75-6

Naked Soled gerbil 69, 75
National Cavy Club 40, 46, 47, 48
National Hamster Council 54, 63
National Fancy Rat Society 102, 103
National Hamster Council Journal 64
National Mongolian Gerbil Society 74, 75
National Mouse Club 79, 86, 87, 89
Netherlands Dwarf rabbit 8, 13, *13*, 24, 27
New Zealand rabbit 16, 17, 27

Outside runs 8, 20, *20*

Peruvian guinea-pig 9, 13, 38, *38*, 39, 41, 47, *47*, 48
Polish rabbit *15*
Pregnancy in
 gerbils 73;
 guinea-pigs 45;
 hamsters 62;
 mice 85;
 rabbits 24-5;
 rats 101
Pro-Rat-A 102
Publications 15, 28, 64, 87, 102

Rabbits 7, 8, 10, 11-34, 36, 38
Rats 10, 93-103
Registration of
 guinea-pigs 46;
 mice 86-7;
 rabbits 27-8
Ring sizes of rabbits 27

Self guinea-pigs 38, 46
Sex determination of gerbils 73;
 guinea-pigs 45, *45*;
 hamsters 61, *61*;
 mice 85;
 rabbits 23-4, *24*;
 rats 101
Show classes for
 gerbils 75-6;
 guinea-pigs 48, 50;
 hamsters 64-5;
 mice 90-1;
 rabbits (Angora) 33

Shows 30, 30-3, 64, 74, 82, 102-3;
 table 30, 48, 89, 90-1;
 pen 30, 48, 90-1
Shows and showing,
 gerbils 74-6;
 guinea-pigs 46-50;
 hamsters 63-5;
 mice 86-92;
 rabbits 26-34;
 rats 102-3
Size, rabbits 8, 16-17, 18, 27
Sleeping quarters for
 guinea-pigs 41;
 hamsters 55;
 mice 82;
 rabbits 18, 19;
 rats 98
Specialist clubs and societies 8, 15, 28, 46-7, 64, 69, 87, 88, 100, 102, 106-7
Standard of perfection 15, 27, 30, 46, 64, 89, 90, 94
Stock-breeding 8, 34, 51, 66, 76, 91-2

Teeth of
 guinea-pigs 35-6, 44;
 hamsters 60;
 rabbits 11-12, 19, 23;
 rats 99, 101
Temperature ranges for
 gerbils 69;
 guinea-pigs 40;
 rabbits 18;
 rats 98
Terms and abbreviations 31-3
Toilet facilities for
 hamsters 55;
 rabbits 8, 12
Tortoiseshell and White guinea-pigs 39, 40, *43*
Toys 53, 57, 70, 93, 99

Varieties *see* Breeds
Veterinary care 10, 23, 44, 84, 101
Vitamin deficiency in
 guinea-pigs 41, 42, 44;
 rabbits 12

Water containers 43, 57, 70-1, 83, 99
Weaning
 gerbils 73;
 guinea-pigs 46;
 hamsters 63;
 mice 85;
 rabbits 26;
 rats 101
White rat *95*